CACTUS CYMRY

INFLUENTIAL WELSH
IN THE
SOUTHERN ARIZONA TERRITORY

BY

JUDE JOHNSON

Published by Open Books Press, USA
www.openbookspress.com

An imprint of Pen & Publish, Inc.
Bloomington, Indiana
(812) 837-9226
info@PenandPublish.com
www.PenandPublish.com

Copyright © 2011 Jude Johnson

All rights reserved.
No part of this book may be reproduced, stored in a retrieval system, or transmitted
by any means, electronic, mechanical, photocopying, recording, or otherwise,
except for brief passages in connection with a review,
without written permission from the author.

ISBN: 978-0-9852737-0-5

This book is printed on acid free paper.

Printed in the USA

Dedication

Am fy nghyfeillion Cymru / For my Welsh friends
Sophie Thomas, Helen Watkins, Ceri Jones, Roy Noble, the
irrepressible Eiry Palfrey,
and Cymry cyber friends on Facebook who've been so kind.
The Welsh always make an impact wherever they travel.
Cymru am byth!

Acknowledgements

To the members of Tucson's only Welsh class and all the members of the Welsh League of Arizona, *diolch yn fawr iawn*—thanks so much for your support all these years.

Alexandria Caster, Kate Reeve, and Christine Saliga helped me find information at the Arizona Historical Society Research Library in Tucson. Nancy Lewis Sosa of History Raiders (http://historyraider.com) and Robert Palmquist are two of the most knowledgeable people alive on the planet today regarding Arizona Territorial history, and I am so grateful for their help and advice.

Special thanks to my circle of writing *amigas*, Gecko Gals Ink: Ashleen O'Gaea, Mary Ann Hutchison, Dewanne Tremont, and Carol Costa for all the encouragement, hugs, and support. Leticia Aros, thanks for all the coffee, *cochitos*, and friendship.

Heartfelt gratitude to Paul Burt and Min Gates of Open Books Press for coming through on short notice. Bravo!

Last but most certainly not least, I want to thank my husband, Roy and son, Parker for their tolerance of my history and writing addictions. No intervention is possible, but if you want to give it a try you could send me to a spa…

Table of Contents

Introduction	ix
What Brought Them Here	1
Arizona Territorial Timetable	7
Samuel Hughes "A Spoon in Every Pot"	13
James Daly "One That Got Away"	31
John S. Williams "Ode to the Common Man"	49
Louis Cameron Hughes "God Has Chosen Me"	53
William M. Griffith "A Recognized Leader"	69
Ben and Lewis Williams "Money Making Mine Management"	75
Other Characters of Note	83
Epilogue	91
Reference Notes	95
About the Author	107

Introduction

Wales—legendary land of poets, choirs, Celts, King Arthur, and Tom Jones—is part of the United Kingdom, aka Great Britain. It is *not* part of England, but a separate nation the same as Scotland and Ireland. People from Wales are *not* "English." British, yes; *English*, no. And many will tell you, the last true Prince of Wales was murdered by the English at the end of the thirteenth century. Llewelyn ap Gruffydd was betrayed by his brother, Dafydd, then ambushed and killed by English soldiers. But then the English king Edward II turned against Dafydd as well. A special execution style was devised for him and subsequent traitors to the crown: to be "hung, drawn and quartered"—strung up by the neck and choked but not to the point of death (which is obviously the "hung" part), then eviscerated carefully to still keep him alive and sensatory while his intestines were thrown onto a fire (the "drawn" part) until definitively dead, then the corpse was hacked into four parts ("quartered") and each section buried in a different locale. Occupational English rule was never especially benevolent so one might understand a wee bit of the Welsh nationalistic resentment.

In the Welsh language, (*Cymraeg—Come-RYEG*) the nation is *Cymru* (*COME-ree*) and its people are *Cymry* (also *COME-ree*). The United States are filled with places with names such as Bryn Mawr ("big hill"), Cardiff By The Sea (California), and a good number of Swanseas. If a name has a preponderance of double Ls, Ws, and Ys, odds are the origins are Welsh. Nearly every state is dotted with chapels built by Welsh Protestants. Numerous Welsh societies across America celebrate their heritage with a *Cymanfa Ganu*, a traditional Welsh hymn sing, or an *Eisteddfod*, a cultural festival with competitions in music, art, and storytelling in *Cymraeg* and English.

But Welsh immigrants in the Arizona Territory never built a single Welsh chapel. They didn't congregate in separate delineated communities as their countrymen did along the East Coast. *Cymry* assimilated quickly out West, marrying Native or Mexican women and abandoning their mother tongue.

Keep in mind as you read this book that in Arizona, all non-Mexican, non-Native, or non-African descended people were (and still are) labeled "Anglo" by residents and officials alike. It has nothing to do with being Anglo-Saxon and everything to do with skin color and "back East" origins. Therefore, many Welsh in Arizona were identified as "Anglo" in newspapers and county documents—as were Swedes, Irish, French, and Germans.

While they did not maintain a distinct and separate identity, *Cymry* in Southern Arizona contributed greatly for good and bad to the growth of Arizona from a dusty, lawless Territory into the cantankerous Forty-Eighth State.

This book is a compilation of research for my historical Western novel, *Dragon & Hawk* and its sequels. It is not meant to be an all-encompassing history, merely a collection of little-known stories and a few wry observations. The scope is generally limited to those who arrived prior to the turn of the twentieth century and the geographical region of Southern Arizona, namely Pima and Cochise Counties.

Jude Johnson
August, 2011

What Brought Them Here

Cactus Cymry

Map of Wales, Original Counties
Courtesy of the Wales National Dept. of Cartography

What Brought Them Here

Why would so many farmers and miners leave their beloved homeland for "a country fit only for Apaches, snakes, and other Queer Reptiles"? One need only look at what was happening in Wales at the turn of the nineteenth century. It wasn't a Happy Place.

From the mid-1700s through 1818, Britain was constantly at war. The Seven Years' War (aka "The French and Indian War"), the American Revolution, another war with America in 1812, and nearly twenty years of the Napoleonic Wars culled the population. Therefore, at the cessation of the Napoleonic Wars, attrition slowed while the birth rate exploded throughout the British Isles. Resources were quickly stripped; malnutrition and starvation ravaged the populace.

Constant warfare had also drained the treasury and created an immense national debt. When a series of severe weather seasons resulted in poor harvests, a great economic depression hit all of Britain hard but devastated Wales. In Pembrokeshire alone, every single bank failed in 1825 and those who had been prudent lost every penny of their savings. No money to buy seed led to fewer harvests and no money to buy goods, leading to a stagnation of commerce, deepening the economic crisis.

Though iron, tin, and coal had been mined and smelted in Britain since Roman times, the expanded utilization of steam engines and industrialization created an insatiable demand for coal. Forced industrialization to obtain coal and iron ore in massive quantities practically enslaved the people of southern Wales, where the high-yield coal mines of Merthyr Tydfil and Pontypridd rapidly ruined the majestic valleys. Children as young as six toiled "down the pit" beside their fathers and mothers until laws enacted in 1842 forbade women and children working in the mines, though many collieries ignored labor laws for decades. In addition, from 1801 through 1840 an influx of immigrants to southern Wales from Ireland, Scotland, middle

England, and Europe arrived to work the mines and ironworks, further straining local resources.

The basic economic structure in farming areas of Britain consisted of aristocratic landed gentry who leased parcels of land to farmers who often paid their rents in crops, livestock, or other goods. Starting in 1793, King George III had to have a yard sale to raise cash (wars are damned expensive business) and released public land for private purchase, but only already landed gentry could afford to buy. This significantly increased and concentrated landlord privileges. As enclosure reduced the amount of available public land to be farmed, rents doubled and tripled over the course of a few years, and then the system moved to cash payment instead of bartered goods. In addition, Each landowner could add tollgates wherever a road crossed or abutted his property to cover the costs for maintenance and repair. Collectors —"Toll farmers"—bid for the privilege to take delivery of these fees. (By 1813, a toll farmer could make as much as £640 per year above and beyond the tolls themselves. That translates loosely to the equivalent of about $50,000 in today's dollars.) There were no standard rates. Soon gates proliferated to the point that there was a toll to pay every three miles. Landlords prospered off beleaguered laborers and farmers. A wide schism gaped between rich and poor with no middle class.

Don't forget religion as a major ingredient of the toxic brew. Between 1790 and 1815 "Poor Laws" increased taxes nearly 400% but passed the responsibility for assisting the poor to parishes of the official Anglican Church. Cash tithes were required from all to fund what relief the Church deigned to bestow, which filled their coffers nicely. Little found its way to the poor. Since nearly eighty percent of the Welsh population was "non-conformist"—i.e., not Anglican, aid was primarily (if still rather grudgingly) given to those who attended "Church" as opposed to "chapel."

What Brought Them Here

Violent riots rocked Wales for nearly a decade. "Chartist" organizations developed through the chapels to work for civil rights. From 1839 till 1845, the *Merched Beca*—Daughters of Rebecca—took inspiration from the Boston Tea Party and organized to destroy toll gates during ever more aggressive acts of civil disobedience that ultimately necessitated the creation of a police force for southern Wales.

Politically, the American Revolution sent cataclysmic waves throughout Europe. Notions of religious freedom and self-determination fueled major dissent among intellectuals. *Cymry* in the colonies figured prominently in the firebrand political machinery of the Revolution; in fact, sixteen Welsh immigrants or American-born Welsh descendants were signers of the Declaration of Independence. As Professor Gwyn Williams in *Beginnings of Radicalism* stated, "In America, radicals freed from inhibition could voice opinions only hinted at in Wales." Their families and admirers back home, inspired by the writings of Thomas Paine and a romanticized revision of Welsh history popularized by Morgan John Rhys, fought for reforms and dreamed of establishing a "New Free Wales" in the West.

It is no wonder then that early 1800s America, with its apparently endless and supposedly empty frontier, appealed to any Welshman dreaming of unbridled freedom.

Arizona Territorial Timetable

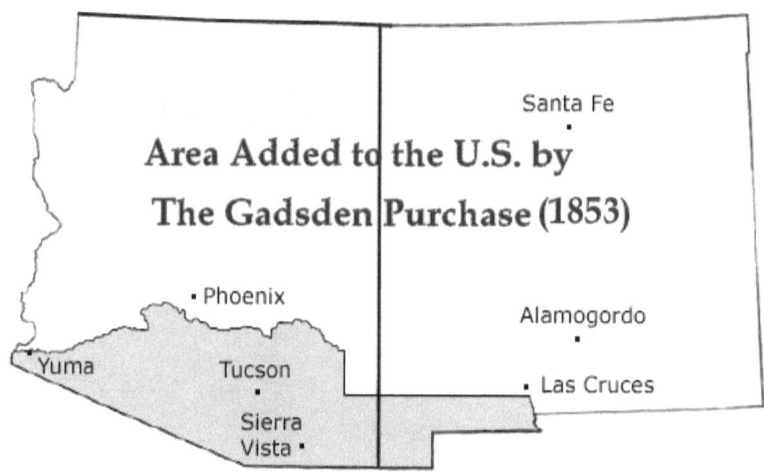

*Areas in New Mexico and Arizona added to the U.S.
with the Gadsden Purchase, 1853
By XcepticZP (Own work) [Public domain],
via Wikimedia Commons*

Arizona Territorial Timetable

1853—The Gadsden Purchase annexes 45,535 square miles of territory into the United States from Mexico. This area encompasses southern New Mexico and Arizona, and includes present day towns of Bisbee, Nogales, Tombstone, and Tucson.

1858—Samuel L. Hughes arrives in Tucson.

1862—March 1, Confederate Army hoists the Confederate Bars and Stars over the pueblo of Tucson, weeks later wins the Battle of Picacho Peak, and retreats May 14 as Union Army approaches from California.

1863—U.S. Government divides the New Mexico Territory and creates the Arizona Territory with Prescott as the capital.

1871—Louis Cameron (L.C.) Hughes arrives in Tucson
   —More than 100 Apache women and children and eight old men are massacred at Camp Grant by vigilantes; additional 28 children are stolen and sold.

1877—Silver, copper, and gold are discovered in the Mule Mountains; Tombstone is founded.
   —L.C. Hughes purchases and establishes *The Arizona Star*, soon to become *The Arizona Daily Star* which is still Tucson's daily newspaper.

1878—William Griffiths relocates to Tucson for his stagecoach line.

1879—Ben and Lewis Williams establish the Copper Queen Mine in Bisbee.

1880 Marshall Williams becomes the Wells Fargo Agent for

Tombstone; backer of the Earp faction in the 1881 gunfight at the OK Corral; suspected of setting up stagecoach robberies.
  —Southern Pacific Railroad arrives in Tucson

1884—John S. Williams, stonecutter, arrives in Tombstone.
  —Samuel Hughes is among founders of the Arizona Pioneer Historical Society

1890—James Daly kills Deputy W.W. Lowther outside of Bisbee.

1893—L.C. Hughes is appointed Arizona Territorial Governor by President Grover Cleveland.

1896—L.C. Hughes is removed from office.

1897—William Griffiths becomes U.S. Marshal in appointed by President William McKinley.

1912—Arizona is granted statehood, becoming the Forty-Eighth State on February 14, 1912.

Arizona Territorial Timetable

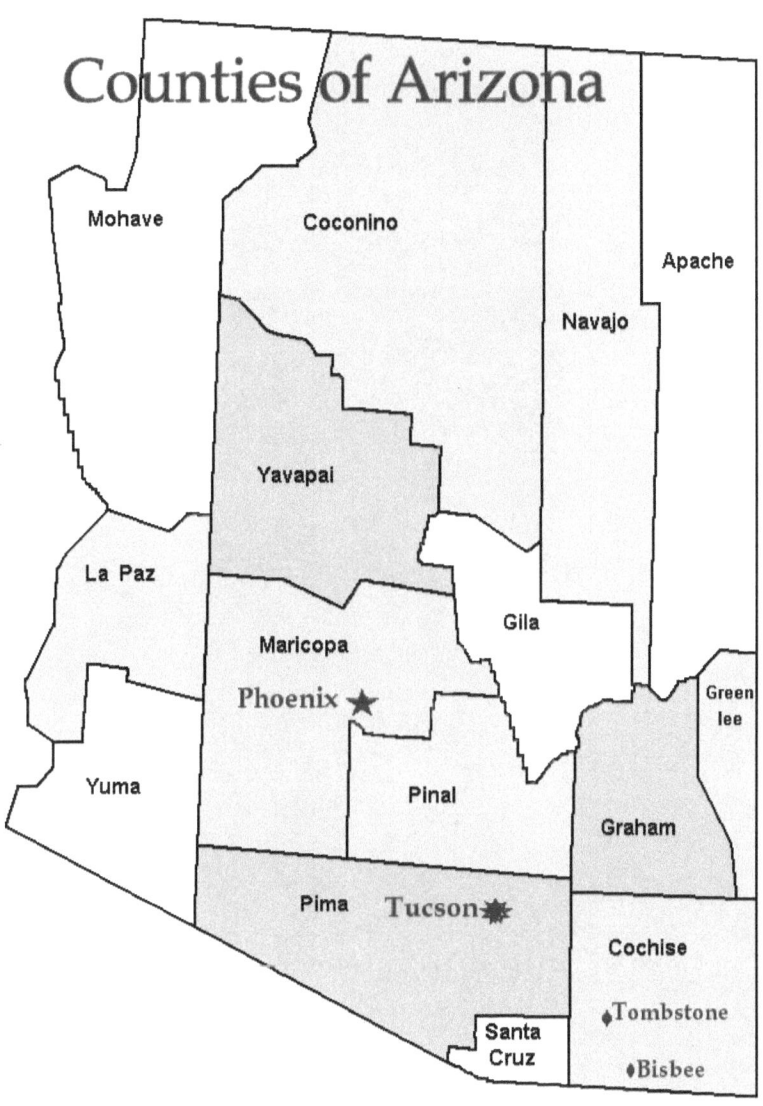

Current Arizona Counties, Cities of interest
Arizona County Map, selfmage graphic by R.Blauert (dk4hb),
via Wikimedia Commons

Samuel Hughes

"A Spoon in Every Pot"

Cactus Cymry

Photo of Sam Hughes neighborhood sign; personal photo

Samuel Hughes

In modern day Tucson, now a city of one million and growing, Sam Hughes Neighborhood is a desirable and historic section of beautiful homes near the University of Arizona. There is an upscale restaurant on the corner of Sixth and Campbell called Sam Hughes Championship Dining. Sam Hughes Elementary School, built in 1927, still educates students in the Tucson Unified School District. A good many Tucsonans, most of whom were not born in Arizona but moved here at some point, have no idea of who Sam Hughes was or what he did to deserve such honorifics from the Anglos who rapidly assumed political control of The Old Pueblo.

It is said the victorious dictate how history is written. Nowhere is that more succinctly demonstrated than with Samuel Hughes: machinist, cook, butcher, banker—and some might claim, water thief and accessory to mass murderer.

That the man possessed a shrewd business instinct or that he was an involved and prominent community leader is never in doubt. Nor did he shy away from touting the attributes of "his town" or his own accomplishments to reporters. That he downplayed and hid his involvement in nefarious dealings and dreadful events demonstrates his formidable skills as a spin master long before the term was conceived. He proudly told his children they were "descended from the Ancient Britons" yet never taught any of them a word of the majestic, ancient language he spoke as a child.

Sam Hughes' Mormon great-grandson Clifford J. Stratton wrote Sam's story to share at a family reunion, tracing the genealogy in meticulous detail, and relating the "rich, oral family history" that he admits "may be a little slanted toward our family's point of view."

One could say it was more of a slippery slope.

Early Days

Samuel Hughes was born 10 April 1829, the third child of Samuel Hughes and Elizabeth Edwards in Pembrokeshire, Wales. Young Sam's mother had a long established family estate in the area of Castell and Clyde in northeastern Pembrokeshire, south of Cardigan. Samuel's father is described as a famer who decided to move the family to Pennsylvania in 1837, "after having been fascinated by the corn sailors brought back from this area. He had a large family and decided the new country seemed like a land of opportunity."

Why a man would pack up his family and not merely leave his farm but his native country and cross the Atlantic Ocean on the basis of looking at some corn is open to speculation (unless it was magic corn enabling reindeer to fly). Only twelve years before, every bank in Pembrokeshire had failed and everyone had lost their entire life savings. Tollgates had proliferated across the country and the *Merched Beca* were getting into high gear of dramatic gate-chopping protests. One version of Sam's "rich oral history" stated that "his paternal grandfather and great-grandfather both bore the name of Samuel, and were the owners of a large estate in Wales." Stratton's account, however, indicates the estate had been in the Edwards family.

Still, both Stratton's account and interviews with Sam in his later years specify "the family retained interest in the estate" back in Wales. Evidently the estate was sold in the 1870s and proceeds divided. Sam says the family thought he'd been killed by Indians and so he did not receive his share of £2,000-£3,200. This was quite a large sum in those days. Stratton states this was likely due to the lack of legal advice Sam would need to pursue his inheritance (despite the fact that his brother Louis C. was a duly licensed, practicing attorney). Sam is quoted as saying, "But we were all the same blood and I could get along without

Samuel Hughes

it." He doesn't mention whether his other siblings felt the same.

As a land owner, father Samuel Hughes might have been seen as a target for the fledgling Daughters of Rebecca, just getting started in their tollgate chopping forays. Or he may have been struggling financially after years of poor harvests, lost savings, and forced payment of tithes, even perhaps facing the prospect of entering the dreaded workhouse.

Either way, America beckoned.

The family immigrated on the "North Star," a sailing vessel whose voyage lasted sixty days. Samuel Hughes began dairy farming (so much for that fascinating corn) at Manayunk, Pennsylvania, in the Philadelphia area in 1837 when Young Sam was but eight years old. The lad spoke with such a heavy Welsh accent that other children made fun of him. He lasted three days in school and never went back.

There is conflicting information about the actual size of the Hughes family. Records show the eldest Hughes children—John, Margaret, Sam, David, William, and Elizabeth—were born in Wales. Some genealogy documents indicate Sallie and Annie Hughes were also born in Wales, but their birth dates are *after* the family immigrated to the United States. It is reasonable to speculate that Sallie Hughes might have been born aboard the "North Star" on the voyage to America, but her headstone indicates she was born in 1838. Annie Hughes is listed as being born in 1840 in Wales, which quite some time after that ship docked in Pennsylvania. Lewis Cameron (L.C.) Hughes (see his chapter) was born in 1842 in Philadelphia. Shortly thereafter, the family moved across the state near Pittsburgh to Allegheny City, where Thomas Hughes was born in 1843. Sam's mother, Elizabeth Edwards, died two months after Thomas' birth.

Clifford J. Stratton (who as a Mormon was quite involved with genealogical research) lists only six Hughes children by Samuel and Elizabeth, yet four other siblings not found in that genealogy are mentioned in the 1901 biography of Sam Hughes; "*David*, a prominent man of New Orleans, La., where his death occurred; Mrs. *Sally (or Sallie)* Taylor and [older sister Lizzie], both residents of DeSoto, Kans.; *William*, who was a member of a Kansas regiment in the Civil war and is now a resident of Lawrence, that state; [Thomas]; and *Annie*, who makes her home in Tucson." *Sallie* and *Annie* are also listed as surviving sisters in Sam's obituary.

Farmer Hughes was severely injured and evidently crippled shortly after Elizabeth's death and was no longer able to provide for his children; it seems further parental contact or involvement with Sam, Louis, or Thomas was not pursued. Evidently he spent some time in the County Poor House in Mount Lebanon, near Pittsburgh, as that was listed as his residence in the 1860 Census. And while it seems Sam encouraged Louis, Thomas, and the aforementioned Annie to come to Arizona once he was established, he made no provisions to move his father, though he certainly had the means. Sam mentions him only in passing, to note that man died at the age of seventy.

By his own account, young Sam began working on a neighboring farm at the age of eleven, an indication of the family's dire straits in their new country. In Allegheny City, he worked driving a canal boat mounted on trucks in sections over the Allegheny Mountains for $6 per month. He made one trip. He and younger brother William were then employed at a cotton factory for $1.25 per week. When Sam's skills making a model wagon were noticed, he was assigned to the blacksmith to make tools. When the factory shut down during a labor strike, Sam hired on at a bakery. With his culinary skills he soon secured a position as a cabin boy on a steamboat plying the Ohio and Mississippi Rivers from Pittsburgh to New Orleans. In 1850 at the age of twenty-one, he signed on as cook with a wagon train headed for the gold fields of California.

Samuel Hughes

During his time in California, Sam Hughes made money far beyond his expectations. He cooked at a hotel for eight dollars a day in gold dust (twice a miner's daily wage) and on the side sold pies, jellies, and gingerbread for $4 per foot square pan. People lined up to buy what he was selling. He then moved on to Sacramento and north to the Rogue River Valley in Oregon, investing in cattle and mine shares, still "gathering nickels."

Sam stated in numerous interviews that he "strained his chest lifting the carcass of a deer onto his horse. Something slipped and he was badly hurt" in 1857 and the doctors told him to seek a warmer climate or he would die. An interesting diagnosis for a strain; generally, those suffering from consumption (TB) were given that dire ultimatum. One account does state Sam Hughes was "compelled to leave California for the milder climate of Arizona, being, at that time, in the last stages of tuberculosis." One must wonder if the "strain" story was a device to deny ever having been labeled a "lunger." Sam had little compassion for those in Tucson's TB sanitarium park: "The lungers will never get well by lying around doing nothing. They want to get interested in something like I did."

In any case, indeed he did seek a warmer climate, selling everything he had for gold. He joined a party of friends headed southeast, aiming ultimately for Texas to purchase cattle. They straggled into the pueblo of *Chúk-son*—the Tohono O'odham (then called the Papago) tribe's name for Tucson—at daybreak on 12 March 1858.

Beginning Anew in The Old Pueblo

At the time of Sam Hughes' arrival, Tucson was primarily a Mexican and Native American *pueblo*. Annexed into the United States by the Gadsden Purchase in 1854, this area that would become Southern Arizona was still part of the New Mexico

Territory and sparsely populated. A presidio (walled enclosure) centered the village, surrounded by small adobe dwellings. Sam set about meeting the few white inhabitants, including Hiram Stevens, his future business partner—and future brother-in-law. There was a dance scheduled for the evening, Stevens told them, so Sam and his friends attended. There he spied a pretty Mexican girl and told Stevens, "I'm going to marry her."

Her name was Atanacia Santa Cruz. She was Hiram Stevens' sister-in-law—and all of seven years old. Atanacia was an orphan. Her older sister and Hiram's wife, Petra Santa Cruz Stevens, and her older maternal aunt, probably saw an opportunity to make sure little Atanacia would be well-cared for when Sam Hughes focused his attentions on the child. By Arizona definition he was "Anglo." He was not a Catholic, but he had gold and obvious unbridled ambition, making him an excellent prospect for a nineteenth century match.

When his friend continued on to Texas, Sam Hughes elected to remain in Tucson. His first business was to set up shop as a butcher. He kept a small herd of cattle near his adobe house outside the presidio, and the business prospered for some time. By 1858 he had invested in silver mines in the Santa Rita Mountains.

But in those few years preceding the Civil War, the majority of white settlers around Tucson were all for seceding from the Union. Congress, afraid of bringing another "slave state" into being, ignored all requests to divide the massive New Mexico Territory and provide settlers with better protection from hostile Indians, solidify their land and mining claims, and bring more law enforcement. In fact, "Secesh" delegates met in Tucson in 1860 to try and form a provisional territorial government all on their own.

When Texas seceded in early 1861, the Union government responded by rescinding the Butterfield Overland Stage

Samuel Hughes

Company's licensed agreement to carry the mail across the Southwest, and sent the order for all Union troops to leave. Small towns and mining camps along the stage route from El Paso to Yuma were suddenly left unprotected. The Apache watched the "blue coats" pack up and roll out, then took full advantage of the opportunity to try and reclaim their lands. The increased Apache attacks heightened the secession debate to a roar.

Sam Hughes was a Henry Clay Whig, and when that party died out, he became a Republican and staunch Union supporter. He liked to tell the story of when Tucson's "Fiery Virginian" William Oury confronted him as the Confederate Army approached the Old Pueblo in late January of 1862: "He told me, 'Get out of town, else we will shoot you.' I said, 'I was here before you were, and I won't go.' And Oury backed down."

Confederate troops rode into town in February. Yet isn't it rather telling that Sam suddenly left Tucson and spent the next few months in California? He entrusted all his business affairs to Hiram Stevens and another partner until word came the Confederates were gone in May. Within three days of his return, he won the Army contract to supply grain to troops, resumed his butchering business, and married not-quite-twelve-year-old Atanacia by the end of that month.

Sam had "waited patiently" for the girl to turn eleven years, nine months old. Even for those times, for a thirty-three-year-old man to take such a young child as his wife was unusual. In all likelihood, her aunt had insisted he at least wait for her to have her first menstrual flow before claiming his "husband's privilege."

Sam steadfastly refused to convert to Catholicism, so he and Atanacia were married in a side chapel at Mission San Xavier del Bac, set amid the Papago settlement ten miles southwest of the presidio of Tucson on 27 May 1862. Her aunt insisted Atanacia wear black as atonement for marrying outside the faith—as though the union had been entirely the child's decision.

Cactus Cymry

Atanacia Santa Cruz Hughes was thirteen years, five months old when her first child was delivered stillborn. The second child was also stillborn, a mere ten months later. She delivered a live baby girl just a few months beyond her fifteenth birthday. Sam and Atanacia had a total of fifteen children. Two were stillborn, three died within three months of birth, and ten reached adulthood.

Atanacia Santa Cruz Hughes, Isabel "Lizzie" Hughes (age two), Samuel Hughes
Courtesy of the Arizona Historical Society, Tucson # 326851

Samuel Hughes

Accessory to a Massacre

Accessory: **n.** *one who helps in the commission of a crime by... providing the weapons, assisting in the planning, providing an alibi, or hiding the principal offender after the crime. Usually the accessory is not immediately present during the crime, but must be aware that the crime is going to be committed or has been committed...a jury or judge may find the accessory just as responsible.*

In 1863, the federal government officially created the Arizona Territory with Prescott as its capital. The end of the Civil War brought more settlers to the Southwest, exacerbating "The Indian Problem." Native Americans, most notably the Apache, vehemently defended their ancestral lands against invading whites. The return of federal troops and the Butterfield Overland Stage operations at the end of the Civil War intensified encroachment on Apache resources. By 1870, Apaches across the Territory were facing starvation.

According to historian Howard Sheldon:

"Atrocities were committed by both the white man and the native Indians. The immigrants, white-eyed enemies or `pindah-lickoyee` as the Indians called them, were moving in by the thousands and exhausting the native food and water resources. The Arivaipa Apaches relied on game and native plants...as their primary food sources. With these problems and a host of others, which included new diseases introduced by the white man, it is easier to understand why the native peoples were unwilling to share their home with these new uninvited guests."

Cactus Cymry

The citizens of Tucson were enraged when Army Lt. Royal Whitman, officer-in-charge of Camp Grant, fifty-five miles north of Tucson and just north of where the Aravaipa Creek meets the San Pedro River, negotiated with the Arivaipa Apache. In February 1871, the Arivaipa chief Eskiminzin had petitioned for peace. Whitman became responsible for handling the surrender of nearly 500 people. He gave permission for about 150 to erect their wikiups under Army protection in the close vicinity of Camp Grant, in essence accepting them as prisoners of war.

However, raids on nearby ranches and settlements continued, resulting in deaths on both sides. The final straw for the settlers of Tucson occurred April 10, 1871 when nineteen head of cattle were stolen. Papagos reported it as the work of Apaches, a posse took chase, and three whites were killed during the pursuit. They killed a lone Indian the Papagos identified as an Arivaipa Apache. When a farmer was killed thirty miles way from Camp Grant a few days later, the Arivaipa Apaches were blamed once again.

One should keep in mind that a number of different Apache tribes were fighting for their lands at that time in Arizona and New Mexico, such as the Mescalero, Chiricahua, and Arivaipa. It is not clear if the Arivaipa were indeed responsible for everything they were blamed for, but the Anglos, Mexicans, and Papagos believed them to be, and the outcome of that is clearly documented.

William "Bill" Oury organized the vigilante raiding party and later bragged about the work he and his group accomplished. Only nine years earlier as a "Secesh," he had threatened to shoot Sam Hughes, yet the two cooperated like old chums on this endeavor. Sam Hughes was Territorial Adjutant General, and provided the guns and ammunition for the six whites and forty-eight Mexicans to attack the Apaches at Camp Grant. Ninety-eight Papago warriors, continual enemies of the Apache, were also recruited. ("Papago" is a derogatory Apache word meaning "bean eater," which is why the tribe finally made an official name change in the 1980s to their own designation for themselves, the Tohono O'odham.)

Numbers vary in the accounting but one thing is clear: more than 110 Arivaipa Apache women, children, and old men were clubbed to death or shot in the predawn darkness on April 30, 1871. An additional twenty-eight babies were abducted to be sold as slaves. At seven-thirty that morning, frantic riders from Tucson's Fort Lowell arrived at Lt. Whitman's quarters to warn him the vigilantes were headed his way. But it was already too late. Camp Grant's surgeon documented the "grisly sight of corpses left to rot in the sun." One lone survivor, a woman who played dead, was finally able to tell the post's Apache interpreters accompanying the surgeon what had happened.

By eight o'clock William Oury and his band were relaxing on the banks of the San Pedro River. That afternoon, Sam Hughes sent a wagon of food and water to meet the victors on the northwestern outskirts of Tucson to celebrate how "swift punishment was dealt out to those red-handed butchers, and they were wiped from the face of the earth."

A letter defending the Arivaipa Apache from Lt. Royal Whitman was published in numerous newspapers back East, and a number of Anglos who had befriended the Apache people and understood their plight campaigned for justice. But such efforts were wasted in Arizona.

In a token show of procedure to appease "East Coast bleeding hearts" and the government, 104 men were put on trial in December 1871 for the atrocities at Camp Grant. The jury of Anglo men returned a verdict of "Not Guilty" for all defendants within nineteen minutes.

It has been said that the Camp Grant Massacre ignited the Apache Wars into the fierce conflagration that would blaze across the Southern Arizona and New Mexico Territories until Geronimo's capture in 1886. It became the American Government's massive attempt at genocide, and it almost succeeded.

Sam Hughes did not go with Oury and his murderous band. He did not physically get blood on his hands. But one could rightly state he hired the hit men, provided the weapons, and then threw them a party for a job well done. One story goes he had Atanacia help make bullets for the men to use. He never once expressed one iota of remorse for the lives of the women and children murdered that morning.

But while Oury remained unashamed of his involvement and even boastful of his actions, defending the slaughter as "swift punishment," Sam Hughes never took responsibility for his generous contribution of guns, ammunition, and food. In interviews given in which he lists all of his accomplishments in "pioneer times"—including hosting in his home Generals Crook and Miles—his financial backing of the atrocity at Camp Grant is never mentioned.

Historian C.L. Sonnichsen writes, "The pioneers deserve to be judged by their own standards and beliefs, not by ours, and in their view…they *had* brought civilization of a sort to the new country and had risked their lives to do it."

But one must consider the same argument has been used to justify genocide throughout the existence of mankind, from the Spanish Inquisition to the Manifest Destiny of the American Frontier to the Nazi Holocaust and ethnic cleansing of Bosnia: "We are bringing Christianity/civilization/order to those inferior to ourselves." If mass murder is an accepted practice, one must question the definition of that "civilization."

The location of the Camp Grant post is now occupied by Central Arizona College. There are no historical markers to indicate its existence or what took place in its shadow.

Samuel Hughes

Water Tolls

Sam Hughes held little bias against non-Apache people. He formed a long-lasting and profitable business partnership with Don Leopoldo Carrillo, one of the more prominent Mexicans in Tucson who foresaw the coming Anglicization of the settlement and decided to throw in his lot with the conquerors. Opportunistic and every bit as ambitious as Hughes, Carrillo owned a number of prime farming parcels along the Santa Cruz River. He was also an inveterate gambler who ran up debts he could not manage.

In 1885, Sam and Leopoldo, along with W.C. Davis, appointed themselves "water commissioners" and built a fence across the Santa Cruz River to control water distribution for Tucson. Perhaps the idea sprang from a distant memory from his childhood. Instead of a "toll farmer" charging to use a road crossing his land, Hughes became a "Water Toll Farmer."

Mexican farmers downstream who by that time had worked the lands for generations suddenly found their fields deprived of vital irrigation unless they paid the commissioners' fees. They sued Hughes and his partners, but by the time Judge F.M. Gregg handed down his decision in the Mexicans' favor of "prior appropriation"—oldest cultivated fields had first rights to water usage—it was too late. Carrillo and Hughes had already achieved what they wanted: the small farms had failed and Hughes had bought their properties for pennies on the dollar, then turned around and leased them to Chinese farmers.

In 1882 the U.S. Exclusion Act limited Chinese males to remain in the country for a maximum of ninety days. They had been barred from working in the mines completely since 1878. Sam Hughes knew he would have a constant turnover of renters and could raise rates as often as he pleased. He was later praised for "providing excellent soil for skilled Chinese farmers."

Yet, Sam did not discriminate against those seeking financial services; business, after all, was business. He built the first bank in Tucson and created mortgages for a number of families, including at least one mixed race couple. Samuel Bostick was a Negro born in Alabama, married to Albina Barraga, born in Sonora, Mexico, who was listed as white in the 1870 Census. On May 1, 1872, Sam Hughes created a mortgage for them for the amount of $330.00 that was discharged by July 1873.

Accomplishing His Goal

Sam Hughes was instrumental in developing businesses and establishing Tucson as a viable town. According to a 1901 glowing summary of his life in a tome praising many Arizona pioneers:

> "He organized the first bank of Tucson, became president of the Santa Cruz bank, and was involved in a number of other financial institutions as a director. Public-spirited and enterprising, he has taken an active interest in the development and upbuilding of his adopted territory, and has done all in his power to advance its welfare. He assisted in organizing the city of Tucson, and was one of its first aldermen, in which office he served for seven years, but refused the mayorship. He was adjutant-general of Arizona six and a half years, and also served as territorial and county treasurer, but when elected to the legislature refused to qualify. He has never sought political honors, preferring to give his undivided attention to his extensive business interests, leaving the offices to those who care more for such positions."

He helped incorporate the pueblo in 1871 and was one of

the founding members of the Pioneer Historical Society formed in 1884. He was the first Mason raised in the Territory, built the First Congregational Church, Santa Cruz Catholic Church, and a Mormon church in Tucson. He was instrumental in getting the Sisters of Saint Joseph to build a convent and offer education for girls. For someone who loudly professed to have no use for book-learning, Sam Hughes made sure his wife and children were provided with opportunity to receive an education, building the schools they would attend in Tucson. He sat on the first Board of Tucson Unified School District which encompassed the entire breadth and width of Pima Country. He financed both the first newspaper in the Territory at Tubac and the Republican-leaning *Tucson Citizen*, though he cautioned Editor John Wasson to never mention his involvement by name.

Poverty was a stern teacher. Sam Hughes learned early that he never wanted to be without money in his pockets, from leaving the Welsh farmland of his childhood on a sailing vessel to scrabbling as an eleven-year-old to help feed his family. He never forgot the value of a nickel, nor did he shy away from trying new enterprises to earn money. He proudly told anyone who would listen, "I had a spoon in every soup."

Sam stated, "I helped build churches and schools and spent my time and my money on them. My hobby was to make a town, I helped get up good school laws...I helped all the churches, one just like another. I have beautiful letters from the pupils of different schools, thanking me for what I did for them." Nowhere does he mention the murdered children and kidnapped babies of Camp Grant. Nor does he mention the children of the Mexican farmers he forced from their land.

And what of the child he wed? Matrimonial interest in a seven-year-old girl nowadays would land him in jail. Even Roman Polanski didn't aim that young. Yet, for Atanacia Hughes, everything she knew from the age of eleven years, nine months came through her husband. He sent her to school in Kansas with five of their children (she finished her thirteenth pregnancy there, successfully delivering daughter Atanacia in Lawrence), provided her with a large home in what was called Snob Hollow of Tucson where all the wealthiest citizens lived, and by all accounts, treated her with affectionate respect.

Samuel Hughes House today, Tucson (Photo by J. Johnson)

The house where Sam and Atanacia lived is still standing and occupied on Main Street. An excellent example of Territorial architecture, the entry is level with the street without a façade or porch, and the west-facing front is shaded with vegetation.

Sam and Atanacia Hughes were married fifty-five years, until his death on 20 June 1917. Yet she is not buried at his side. Because she was a devout Roman Catholic all her life and Sam remained a steadfast nonconformist Protestant, Atanacia Santa Cruz Hughes (who died on 12 November 1934) is buried in the Catholic Diocese's Holy Hope Cemetery in Tucson. Samuel Hughes is buried in Evergreen Cemetery, with hundreds of graves and a concrete arroyo between him and his wife.

James Daly

"One that Got Away"

Welsh Miners of the Copper Queen, circa 1884
Courtesy of History Raiders Research

James Daly

There is a touristy tale oft told in Tombstone of an Irish miner enamored of a certain "soiled dove" who worked in the brothel in The Birdcage Theater. The story goes that the miner left his claim called "The Irish Meg" to the woman when he died, which she sold and used the proceeds to move to New York and open a successful hotel. It is another of those Tombstone stories based on an iota of truth and a liberal dose of error, exaggeration, and fabrication.

Firstly, The Birdcage Theater never officially housed a brothel. A claim registered as the Irish *Mag* did indeed exist—but not in Tombstone. The miner also really existed. However, he was not Irish. He was a cantankerous, paranoid Welshman named James Daly.

Just because you're paranoid doesn't mean they aren't out to get you.

Daly is listed as living with his family in Cardiff, Glamorganshire, at age seven in the 1851 Census of Wales. By age twenty, he is a naturalized citizen of the United States. By 1884, he is in Cochise County's Great Registry with his occupation stated as miner. By 1890 he's accused of committing "one of the most celebrated crimes in the annals of Arizona history."

It all started back in 1877 when the first discoveries of copper and silver ores were made by soldiers chasing Apaches through the high mountain passes just north of the Territory's border with Mexico. One claim passed from an Army scout named Jack Dunn to a man named Hugh Jones [a Welsh name if ever there was one, but there is no further information about him anywhere other than the mention of his name] who abandoned his discovery because he saw nothing more than "copper-stained rock". Once a small smelter was built and the concentration of copper ore was determined to be twenty-four to twenty-six percent—the richest in North America—prospectors swarmed the county in a wide swath between the railroad depot at Benson and the Mexican border.

No one mineral is ever the sole component in a lode of ore. Copper is found with malachite, lead, silver, and gold. By 1880, silver mines ran under nearly every street in Tombstone, creating the boom that defined the town and gave rise to many an Old West legend and myth. The Mule Mountains outside Bisbee were soon crisscrossed with claims and denuded of trees to fuel smelter furnaces.

Copper demand rocketed from Eastern cities wiring for electricity and the advancement of telegraph lines across the Southwest. It was a wild, exciting time for prospectors hoping to strike it rich.

The most famous claim in Arizona was the Copper Queen Mine. The original prospect claim was purchased by John Ballard and William Martin of San Francisco. They were not wise to the ways of mining, but were financial partners with DeWitt Bisbee, a brother-in-law of Ben and Lewis Williams. (DeWitt S. Bisbee is the town's namesake, though he never set foot in the place. See the chapter on Ben and Lewis Williams.) The Williams brothers managed the Copper Queen well, eventually developing it into one of the largest and most profitable copper mines in the United States, responsible at its peak for more then thirty percent of the nation's supply.

In 1881 Dr. James Douglas, a Scotsman metallurgist working for Phelps, Dodge and Company out of New York, came to Bisbee from the company's copper mining operations in Morenci. He obtained an option on a claim called the Atlanta, right next to the Copper Queen.

Douglas hit the main Atlanta lode in 1884, at almost the same time that a Copper Queen tunnel penetrated the lode from a different spot. Arizona mining operations at the time stuck strictly to the "rule of the apex," according to which a claim

James Daly

owner could follow a vein of ore onto another claim, if the deposit had come closest to the surface on his land.

Ballard and Martin wrongly assumed the Copper Queen had played out. Rather than continue to battle through certain litigation with Phelps-Dodge's Atlanta claim, they sold the Queen. The two mines became the Copper Queen Consolidated Company in 1885, retaining the Williams brothers as managers.

Douglas, considered the "moving spirit" behind all of Phelps, Dodge and Company's operations in the Territory, wasn't satisfied with simply combining the Atlanta and Copper Queen mines. He assumed other outlying claims could tap into ore loads the Copper Queen was working, threatening the same sort of proprietary problems that he'd had with the Atlanta. He was right. The Copper Queen took a massive legal hit at the hands of the adjoining Arizona Prince claim in an apex or extralateral rights case that the Queen lost. That's when Douglas decided to "obliterate the law of the apex" by either buying up adjoining claims or making sideline agreements with them, in which both sides pledged to refrain from exercising those extralateral rights. Once that was arranged, Douglas vigorously pursued acquisition of outlying claims to expand the Copper Queen's territory, buying out the Goddard, Neptune, and Lowell mining groups for Phelps-Dodge.

Then Douglas hit a granite wall named James Daly, owner of the Irish Mag (not "Meg") claim.

Known for his short and violent temper as well as legendary obstinacy, James Daly could be physically imposing. He stood six feet tall when the average man stood five-foot-five, and his violent nature was already known around Bisbee. The reputation of miners from Wales to start a fight without warning simply for entertainment was already well-established; Daly did his best to live up to the hype.

As Dr. James Douglas and Phelps-Dodge gobbled smaller companies and annexed their claims, Daly grew anxious. When

35

he refused to sell the Irish Mag, small annoyances suddenly increased in frequency and fueled his paranoia. Someone cut timber from his property, once, twice, and again. Daly confronted Mexican trespassers and learned they were workers from the Copper Queen. He filed complaints, told anyone and everyone he was being harassed, but nothing changed.

Then he learned that Phelps-Dodge planned to build the Arizona & Southeastern Railroad to pass over his claims, allowing them to condemn his property and lower its value. Daly was incensed.

Bisbee Constable Dan Simmons was assigned to serve a summons of condemnation suit. Daly might have been paranoid but he certainly wasn't stupid; he knew if he did not personally receive the papers in hand, the suit could not proceed. So he ran from his shack as soon as he saw the constable heading his way. Simmons, in his great excitement and determination to serve the summons, shot at Daly and hit him in the ankle. Convicted of shooting an unarmed man, Simmons was sent to Yuma Territorial Prison for several years.

But James Douglas was nothing if not determined to get what he wanted for Phelps-Dodge. Whether he had actually hired workers to harass James Daly into selling the Irish Mag claim or not, he continued to press for a declaration of condemnation of Daly's property.

By April of 1890, Daly had had enough of Copper Queen workers cutting his timber without his permission and initiated a fistfight with a couple of Mexican men on his property. W.W. Lowther was the new constable faced with the prospect of serving a warrant on Daly for assault. Lowther had served one term as Sheriff in Gila County, and had also been a miner. Described as "a big, easy going fellow, brave though discreet, a man who above all others could serve a difficult process without a row," Lowther had a reputation of being a calming influence in the rough and tumble saloon brawls of Bisbee's Brewery Gulch. He knew of Daly and had heard of his quick temper.

What happened next is reported as through an eye witness, though no one was physically present: "Suddenly, through a window came a flash and a report and Lowther fell, shot through the heart by an unseen assassin. When found, the murdered officer still had between his teeth the toothpick he had been chewing when so suddenly stricken."

Six weeks after Lowther's death, this notice was printed in *The Arizona Republican* newspaper:

> W.W. LOWTHER
> On the eleventh day of April last, W.W. Lowther, Deputy Sheriff of Cochise County was brutally murdered by James Daly near the town of Bisbee. The murderer escaped. The local authorities at once offered a reward, the following reward being issued by the Copper Queen Consolidated Mining Company:
>
> "Twenty five hundred dollars reward is hereby offered by the Copper Queen Consoli-dated Mining Company and the citizens of Bisbee for the arrest and conviction or positive proof of the death of James Daly, who murdered W.W. Lowther, near Bisbee, on the afternoon of Friday, April 11, 1890. Daly is a man apparently 50 years of age, although in reality several years younger, six feet in height, found face, slightly pockmarked, sandy complexion, red moustache, weight about 190 pounds, scar on foot and also a scar across the neck made by a pistol shot. Speaks with a strong Welsh accent.
>
> Sheriff Slaughter of Cochise County offered an additional reward of $500.

They forgot to add, "Walks with a limp."

Three thousand dollars was a great deal of money in 1890. But Daly escaped, hidden and helped by miner friends as John Slaughter, the infamous "Wicked Little Gringo" sheriff of Cochise County, pursued the Welshman to Morenci, a copper mining town near the New Mexico border. Daly managed to escape the Arizona Territory, yet contacted a saloon keeper named Andy Mehan to tend to his holdings in Bisbee.

Then Mehan went bankrupt. A letter supposedly written by Daly giving Mehan his properties for $100 was used as evidence to distribute those properties to creditors; the Irish Mag claim went to a man named Adolph Cohn. Complications arose when a German woman appeared in Bisbee in June 1894, claiming to have married James Daly in Leadville, Colorado in 1877. She said they had lived together there, raising twin sons, until the Welshman abandoned her in May 1880 to come to Bisbee.

However, the German woman disappeared as soon as another woman stepped forward as Daly's wife. Angela Diaz, an attractive Mexican woman, had lived with Daly for five years in Bisbee and had even fronted the money for him to file titles on the Irish Mag and other claims. Unfortunately, when Daly escaped, he abandoned Angela to fend for herself. Having helped file the titles to the property, she considered it hers by default. She then sold the Irish Mag and the rest of Daly's property to a man named Martin Costello for $1800.

The contentions of who owned what began in District Court when Costello contested the creditor Cohn. The legal ramifications of defining what constituted a valid deed and transfer of proprietary rights made this one of Arizona's most important—and longest—court battles. The case went all the way to the Supreme Court of the United States, a rarity for Territorial disputes.

A History of American Mining describes the situation thusly:

"Eventually the Supreme Court of the United States recognized [Diaz's] title, which ...passed to Martin Costello of Tombstone. He was willing to sell for $500,000, and [Phelps-Dodge representative James] Douglas was willing to take a bond at that price provided he could explore the property by extending the underground workings of the Copper Queen mine, whereas Costello insisted that the work be done from the surface of the Irish Mag, so that he would have a shaft in case the deal fell through. When these negotiations failed, in 1901, the Irish Mag was purchased by a group of gentlemen from Michigan and Pennsylvania in the name of the Lake Superior & Western Development Company..."

James Daly had successfully held out against a Scotsman every bit as stubborn as himself, and forced the burgeoning corporate giant Phelps-Dodge Company to eventually pay far more for the Irish Mag than if they had simply offered him fair market value in 1890. True, he didn't see a penny of it, but he may have enjoyed a bit of Welsh *schadenfreude*: *fel mêl yn y bis* (literally "like honey on the fingers," the sweetly delicious satisfaction one feels when an enemy suffers) when he heard of the litigious gyrations Douglas and the Company were embroiled in over the Irish Mag.

James Daly was never brought to justice for the murder of W.W. Lowther. His whereabouts remained veiled in uncertainty and rumor. He supposedly died in San Francisco in 1895, but could truthfully brag that for as long as he lived, the Copper Queen Mining Consortium would never possess the Irish Mag.

John S. Williams

"Ode to the Common Man"

*John S. Williams, former mayor of Bisbee
(fourth from left and inset)
Courtesy of the Arizona Historical Society, Tucson #3784*

John S. Williams

There is something to be said for men who spend their lives quietly taking care of their communities and families. No one celebrates their birthdays with fanfare and fireworks. Once they pass on, quite often any of achievements they may have accomplished are forgotten. But men such as these are the backbone of a stable society.

One such man was a stonecutter named John S. Williams. Born in 1849, he was twenty-two, married to Mary Thomas, and living in Clase Lower Llangyfelach, Glamorganshire, according to the 1871 Census of Wales. In 1880, he became a naturalized citizen of the United States in San Luis Obispo, California. By 1884 he and his wife are included in the Great Registry of Cochise County, living in Bisbee.

There are no tales of heroism or scandal about John S. Williams. He didn't create any miraculous stone-cutting innovations, nor did he perform any great feats of renown. He and his wife had no children. But he was one of Bisbee's first mayors, living in the area known as Tombstone Canyon, knapping out grave markers and cornerstones with dignified craftsmanship. He saw the Territory become a state in 1912 and it is quite probable he proudly cast his first vote in a presidential election that November. He died in 1926 at the age of seventy-seven. His grave in Bisbee's Evergreen Cemetery is marked with large granite headstone.

John S. Williams' life of steady work and community involvement was part of the mortar that helped to build a Territory into one of the United States brick by brick.

Here's to the stonemason, no longer totally unremarked and underappreciated.

John S. Williams gravestone, (Photo by J. Johnson)

Louis Cameron Hughes

"God Has Chosen Me"

The Hon. Governor L.C. Hughes, 1893
Courtesy of the Arizona Historical Society, Tucson #B67585

"No man ever earned a more honorable title than that given to Louis C. Hughes by the people of Arizona, among whom he is known as the 'state builder.' The name has been conferred upon him in grateful recognition of his many years of steadfast and faithful labor along lines of state organization, improvement, development and reform and in appreciation of the constructive work he has accomplished along public and semi-public lines. His reward has been the honor, esteem and gratitude of the people he served and the privilege of witnessing the growth and continued development of the great commonwealth of Arizona."
—from *Arizona The Youngest State*, 1916

Ask anyone on the streets of modern day Tucson about Louis "L.C." Hughes and their response will be, "Who?" Unlike his brother Sam Hughes, there are no neighborhoods, parks, schools, or buildings named or a man so idolized in 1916. He has been nearly erased from the city and state's collective memory.

Early Days

Biographies of Samuel and L.C. Hughes suffer from a few different inconsistencies in family information. Sam's states his family immigrated in 1837 while L.C.'s maintains they arrived in 1840. The number of siblings varies from nine to seven, and L.C. never mentions any but Sam by name.

There can be no doubt that Louis Cameron Hughes' childhood was less than idyllic. Born on May 15, 1842 in Philadelphia Pennsylvania, he was the penultimate child of Samuel and Elizabeth Hughes. Shortly after his birth, the family moved more than 300 miles west to Allegheny City in the Pittsburgh area. Louis was fourteen months old when his mother, Elizabeth

Edwards Hughes, died eight weeks after the birth of his younger brother, Thomas. His father was either severely injured or crippled in 1844. L.C. and Thomas were sent to the Orphan Asylum in Allegheny County, Pennsylvania, while siblings Sallie, William, and David were each placed with different families. Older brother John had died in 1840 and Sam had already left for the California gold fields that year. Mysterious older sister Annie isn't mentioned anywhere until the 1880 Census, when she is included in both Sam and Thomas' households in Tucson and described as "refused to give immigration status."

Louis became an indentured servant at age ten to devout Calvinist farmer Samuel Alter. One can safely assume the doctrines first promoted by John Calvin (1509-1564) were ingrained (if not beaten as was common during those days) into the young boy's head on a daily basis. That theology espoused "God is sovereign, has made all choices and man therefore, has no free will and no control over his life and destiny, that God has unconditionally chosen some people to be saved who cannot be lost regardless of their actions, and those not so chosen are unavoidably sentenced to hell regardless of their behavior. To bring about man's salvation, the Holy Spirit moves the chosen few toward God, thereby condemning the rest to eternity in hell. These chosen people can not resist God's grace and, therefore, cannot be lost or become lost."

It is quite probable L.C. Hughes felt "called to God's Glory" early in his life. Religion drove his every action. Perhaps he felt he was indeed one of The Elected and as such could do no wrong; he was preordained to be saved and could never lose that salvation. Imagine the incredible sense of self-righteousness that would engender. By most accounts, Louis certainly suffered no lack thereof.

L.C.'s interviews say he was released from his indentured servitude at age sixteen, "given $15 and sent out into the world."

Louis Cameron Hughes

Yet the 1860 Census—when he would have been eighteen—still counts him as part of Farmer Alter's household.

Math skills evidently were not a priority for the Hughes brothers when it came to their biographical information. But throw a nickel into the equation and neither erred.

L.C. attended public school in Meadville, Pennsylvania, where "the orphan boy had read Uncle Tom's Cabin, and taking part in the school debates, was ardent for the freedom of black boys and girls." Perhaps his indentured servitude gave him insight into what slavery must have been like, engendering compassion and sympathy to the Negro experience, but he had little to none for people of other races once he arrived in Arizona.

Enlisting in the 101st Regiment of Pennsylvania Volunteers at Pittsburgh on 30 September 1861, L.C. jumped into the Union Army a mere five months after the Confederate attack on Fort Sumter in South Carolina officially started the Civil War. His small stature—five-foot-five-inches tall—had thwarted his two previous attempts to enlist, and though he signed up for three years, Louis was discharged in North Carolina after eighteen months due to a life-threatening case of dysentery. He returned to Pennsylvania, started working as a machinist, soon was accepted as a journeyman, and joined Machinists and Blacksmiths' Union No.2 of Pittsburgh. Working through the union, he eventually secured a petition of several thousand workingmen of Pittsburgh "sent to Congress to help pass the first eight-hour workday law in the United States." He saved his pay and enrolled in Meadville Theological School, indicating his thirst for continued religious comprehension.

Louis also attended Edinboro State Normal School, studied law, and met Miss E. Josephine Brawley, a Wesleyan Methodist of strong conviction and purpose. The Methodist preference for rational study of Scripture and reason in all decisions evidently appealed to his fervent love of organization. Miss Brawley's friends included Frances Willard and Susan B. Anthony, fanatic activists in the labor, temperance, and women's suffrage movements. L.C. and Josephine were married in July of 1868, and that year he delivered an address on "Trades-Unions, Their Cause, Influence and Present Necessity" before the International Convention of Machinists and Blacksmiths' Union of America and Great Britain, at Cleveland, Ohio.

Law and unions were Hughes' passion; he threw himself into his practice to the point of physical exhaustion and "his seeking rest and absence from the fretting and agitating multitude." At his brother's invitation, he and Josephine moved to the Arizona Territory in 1871, where she was the third "American woman"—i.e., white—to become a permanent resident of Tucson. Prior to the 1870s, Anglo men frequently married *Mexicanas* and Native women. But once white women from the East came in larger numbers with their Victorian expectations of family and religion, racial bias and discrimination took root and flourished throughout the Territory like weeds after a brushfire.

Territorial Crusades

Louis and Josephine were evangelical Christians, determined from the moment of their arrival to correct all the wrongfulness of Territorial life: battling to close saloons, gambling establishments, and brothels, while bringing Protestant Enlightenment to the Spanish-influenced, traditionally Roman Catholic population. The new Mrs. Hughes was so fervent in her Methodist faith she refused social interaction with her much younger sister-in-law, Atanacia Hughes. At least that is the official family explanation, which fails to mention the high probability that the brown color of Atanacia's skin was also a major factor.

> Mr. Hughes was...placed at the head of the first daily and...the paper became a power in the territory. In its

second issue it declared a new policy for the treatment of the Apache Indians, the criminal element of which had caused constant disturbance and brought terror among the residents of the territory...The citizens were unable to mete out to them the punishment their cruelties deserved. Believing the only remedy was to remove the worst element of these Indians entirely from the territory, Mr. Hughes went to Washington, presented the matter fully to President Cleveland...

It was L.C. who advocated banishing captured Apaches to Florida, removing them from their ancestral homelands and stripping them of their cultural identity even in death, for their bodies were not to be returned to Arizona. Generals Crook and Miles were routinely entertained at Louis and Josephine's home throughout the Apache wars. One can only imagine the spirited discussions that ensued.

Crook, in his two tours of duty in A.T., 1871-1875 and 1882-1886, attempted to negotiate when he could, fought when he had to, then supported the Apaches and other tribes in their efforts on the reservations established during his first tour. He urged Indian citizenship, which must have appalled Josephine Hughes into near apoplexy. Louis didn't really want justice for the Apaches; he likely saw himself as an "Avenging Angel" bent on inflicting "the punishment their cruelties deserved." Yet, whatever backlash had finally resonated from the Camp Grant Massacre in 1871 seems to have prevented him from advocating total annihilation.

When the Chiricahua scouts who had tracked Geronimo for the U.S. Army were summarily dismissed and shipped off to Florida just the same as those they had helped capture, Crook was outraged. He did what he could before his fatal heart attack in 1890 to get them returned.

Nelson A. Miles, who succeeded Crook as Department Commander in 1886, initially protested the 1886 deportations then decided removal of the Apaches was the better course—to keep Geronimo and his band from either being mobbed and lynched, or tried in a Territorial court with the almost certain equivalent of a legal lynching.

Still, Louis' influence at the time was significant, and Geronimo was never permitted to return to his homeland. He was buried at Fort Sill, Oklahoma upon his death in 1909. According to lore, members of Yale's secret society Skull and Bones—including Prescott Bush, former President George W. Bush's grandfather—dug up Geronimo's grave when stationed at the fort as Army volunteers during World War I. A purported diary of the event, sent to a leader of the San Carlos Apache tribal nation in the 1980s by an anonymous Bonesman, records Geronimo's skull and other remains were taken from the leader's burial site. Officials at Fort Sill deny the grave was ever disturbed, but at the time of this writing in 2011, Geronimo's descendants are still fighting to have his remains returned for traditional Apache burial in the Gila wilderness of eastern Arizona.

L.C. Hughes also increased the number of Indian industrial schools, "training Arizona Indian children in the territory, for the conservation of their health and to enable them to learn local industrial pursuits." Such schools endeavored to eradicate all traces of Native belief and culture out of these children, rendering them incapable of returning to live among their own people. Their skin color kept them from assimilating into the increasingly prejudiced white society which now controlled the Territory, so they belonged nowhere. Most spent their lives in misery. Many committed suicide.

All trials of Indians were removed from local territorial jurisdiction to federal court through L.C.'s efforts, and according to James H. McClintock, "recommendations were made for appropriation for irrigation of lands of the Indian reservations; setting a part for allotment lands for Indians wishing to take them in severalty, especially the Papago, Maricopa, Pima and the Yuma tribes; denying ground water access to hostiles," but documentation to confirm such claims has eluded this author.

Hughes then worked on the creation of a federal court "for the settlement of Mexican and private land grant titles [which] resulted in the invalidation of claims to more than twelve million, five hundred thousand acres of land in Arizona and in the return of this immense tract to the public domain." The U.S. Court of Private Land Claims was to give effect to the provisions of the Treaty of Guadalupe Hidalgo that called for the validation of properly-proven Mexican land claims (the land grants). Indications are that the Court actually functioned in a painstaking and scrupulous manner in reviewing thousands of pages of documents and testimony, sorting fact from fantasy.

L.C. Hughes was admitted to practice law before the Arizona Territorial Supreme Court on January 17, 1873. He was a city councilman for Tucson in June of 1872 and appointed a county attorney; a probate judge and ex-officio county superintendent of schools; served as district attorney two terms; United States court commissioner; a member of the board of the World's Fair Commission at Chicago for Arizona; and delegate to the national democratic conventions in 1884 and 1892.

He also served as Attorney General of the Arizona Territory for a short period in 1874. Letters published in the *Tucson Citizen* appeared to indicate Hughes and "some agent of the government" colluded to blackmail two men named Charles Lesinsky and E.M. Pearce. Territorial Governor A.P.K. Safford, never what L.C. would call a friend, then sent a letter to be published in the *Citizen* demanding an explanation or else he would have no choice but to insist upon his resignation for official misconduct. L.C. "declined to prematurely present any statement of my case because that would subject it to disparaging comment without any possible service to truth or justice." Safford then demanded he resign as both Notary Public and Attorney General, and L.C. did. No charges were filed, no trial was conducted, but those letters were fodder against Hughes for decades.

In March of 1877, L.C. bought what would soon become *The Arizona Daily Star*, Arizona's first daily newspaper. *The Star* served as L.C.'s pulpit for thirty years, and polarization became his forte. Employees were emphatically encouraged to practice temperance, and his wife (as business manager) changed the payday schedule from Saturday to Monday to thwart men from spending their money on alcohol.

As a liberal Democrat, Hughes used his paper to endorse women's suffrage, the secret ballots, and labor unions. Laws on prostitution, furnishing liquor to minors, punishing adultery, and the following of the Sabbath law were all being ignored. In his opinion, strict Christian law should have been strictly enforced upon every inhabitant of the Territory. His notion of righteousness would have been akin to a Christian Taliban.

Hughes was elected the first president of the Arizona Press Association when it was created in 1892. The heyday of yellow journalism in the late nineteenth century played both for and against him.

L.C. Hughes was appointed Territorial Governor of Arizona by President Grover Cleveland in 1893. "He Has Got It" the Republican-based *Tucson Citizen* crowed and claimed with a backhanded compliment, "This is what The Citizen has always said would be the case and all who have opposed him had now better make the best of a bad job. Mr. Hughes will fill the office in as good a style as any man in the Democratic Party."

His administration accomplished the first reduction of Territorial government indebtedness in fifteen years. He also reduced the amount of money spent maintaining prisons and the insane asylum by eliminating a number of board positions and administrators, creating a great deal of bitter enmity. He enacted parole laws and required convicts to work. Hughes' maxim: "Savages can not be civilized, nor criminals reformed, without labor." While in office, he also established the Flagstaff and Tempe Normal Schools (now Northern Arizona University and Arizona State University, respectively) and saw the first dormitory built at the University of Arizona in Tucson. He infuriated a number of people by enacting liberal land conservation legislation such as setting aside the Petrified Forest as a national park.

During his tenure as Governor, L.C. turned over administrative and editorial control of *The Arizona Daily Star* over to his wife, Josephine. This was not a popular move. L.C. saw his wife as his partner in all things and treated her accordingly. They had three children: daughter Gertrude, daughter Josephine who died at age two, and son John T. Hughes, who later went on to become one of the first State Senators. In fact, John T. Hughes introduced the enfranchisement bill that gave women in Arizona the vote in November 1912, eight years before the rest of the United States.

His land management and other liberal policies, cutting state administrative jobs, and scathing editorials critical of federal resistance to those policies written by his wife as acting editor of *The Arizona Daily Star*, enticed President Cleveland to remove him from office in April of 1896. L.C. returned to running his newspaper in Tucson and could often be encountered on the streets preaching temperance with the Salvation Army. He served on the Arizona Board of Regents in administering the state educational institutions and advocated allowing students to work in various departments to help pay for their education.

However, L.C. Hughes had his greatest success in creating political and personal enemies in the Tucson community. The *Tucson Citizen* ran this editorial on May 22, 1905, beside reprints of the 1874 letters between L.C. and Governor Safford:

Skinning a Skunk

L.C. Hughes, commonly and popularly known as Pinhead Hughes, takes up two recent miscarriages of justice on which to base some Sunday Reflections. It is hardly necessary to say that Pinhead approves of the miscarriages of justice. Miscarriages of justice have kept Pinhead out of the penitentiary and he is able to absorb the human feeling of putting himself in the offender's place.

It is really a waste of time to take any notice of any utterance of Pinhead Hughes. No man ever resided in any community so thoroughly overwhelmed with the contempt of the community as is the lot of Hughes. No man believes anything that he says. No man or woman believes that he is honest. He has sought and taken bribes. He has turned traitor to all policies that he preached. He has sold out friends and accepted rewards from enemies. He has been kicked and cuffed and slapped and battered and put upon until a full grown man feels ashamed to subject him further to physical chastisement. He has disgraced manhood with cowardice and a depravity that is worse than cowardice. He had disgraced the profession of the law with chicanery and efforts to blackmail. He has disgraced public office with corruption and extortion. He has disgraced journalism with shams and swindles ranging all the way from discreditable to felonious. His life is a lie, his example a plague; venality and depravity the sources of his being, and physical wretchedness his defense and palladium.

> There is no man or woman in the community too vile to become the purchaser and user of Hughes for the time being. He has neither courage, character nor convictions. He is despised by those who use him and has only the contempt of those who observe him.
>
> The whole record of Pinhead Hughes whether as man, husband, brother, father or friend is a dull monotony of baseness that it would puzzle hell to reproduce or Omnipotence to duplicate. As was said in a great presence by another these are severe words such as no good man would deserve, such as no brave man would bear. We are aware, too, that is proved to be untrue, they are libelous.

Pundits on MSNBC and Fox News today pale in comparison. One should also keep in mind that staunch Republican Sam Hughes was a secret financial backer of the *Citizen*. There appears to be little love lost between L.C. and the rest of the Hughes family. While a *Tucson Citizen* interview with Sam in 1915 quotes L.C. speaking well of his brother, it seems the favor was never returned.

L.C. Hughes' influence had waned greatly by the turn of the twentieth century. He sold *The Arizona Daily Star* in 1907 when a libel suit was filed against him, and retired from public life. With wife Josephine, he remained steadfast in the temperance movement supporting Prohibition; so much so that when he was invited by President Theodore Roosevelt to attend the christening of the U.S.S. Arizona in June 1915, he refused to attend because champagne would be used in the ceremony. (As a point of historical significance, this was indeed the same battleship sunk by Japanese bombers on December 7, 1941. The still-seeping wreckage now serves as the foundation of the Pearl Harbor Memorial in Honolulu.)

Louis Cameron Hughes died of pneumonia November 24, 1915 and is buried in Evergreen Cemetery in Tucson. A small, flat granite placard marks his grave, unlike the monumental tombstone marking his brother Sam's. Both he and his wife alienated so many Tucsonans in their lifetime that not one structure, library, or water fountain is named for them or their children in the city. Their house at No.158 Court Street, once described as "one of the historic landmarks of the state" was demolished to create a park near the Pima County Courthouse. There is no placard, plate, or historical marker at the site.

The legacy of L.C. Hughes continues to stir anger. Native people have had to fight long and costly court battles to have their ancestors' remains returned to their homeland. His definition of "love of neighbors and a passion for justice" applied to former slaves and Anglos, yet exempted Native Americans and Mexicans.

His newspaper, the *Arizona Daily* Star, continues to espouse liberal Democratic endorsements, but is no longer locally owned. (As a side note, the *Star* remains in circulation; the *Tucson Citizen* closed its doors and now exists only online.)

There is no question Louis Cameron Hughes contributed greatly to the institutions of education in Arizona, women's suffrage, the revocation of legalized prostitution and gambling, and decrease of excessive graft in Territorial government. After all, he when he came into office the territorial treasury was facing a deficit of more than fifty thousand dollars; at the close of 1894, Arizona had its first surplus in more than fifteen years—and this result with no increase of taxation. He provided Territorial citizens with current news via the first daily paper in Arizona, and vigorously promoted Arizona for settlement and statehood.

There is also no question he was instrumental in the near genocide of the Apache people, deprived thousands of Mexicans and Native Americans of their land, had his own definitions of blackmail and extortion, and imposed strict notions of temperance and Christianity upon as many people as he could despite the First Amendment of the U.S. Constitution.

It is up to the reader to decide whether the progressive ideas outweigh his repressive actions.

William M. Griffith

"A Recognized Leader"

U.S. Marshal of Arizona William M. Griffith
Courtesy of the Arizona Historical Society, Tucson #70932

William M. Griffith

A farmer and Quaker named Abel Griffith emigrated from Wales during the turbulent early nineteenth century to Westchester, Pennsylvania. Abel was successful at farming in the New World enough to send his son, Thomas, to college in Philadelphia. Thomas became a Baptist minister, married an English woman named Jane Hare, and started his family as he preached in Westchester and Hepzabaugh, Pennsylvania. The eldest of his four children, William M. Griffith, was born on April 14, 1839.

William Griffith embodied the spirit of those who flocked to the West. A firm believer in the Union, he fought in the Civil War in the Army of the Southwest out of Missouri, surviving the battles of Lookout Mountain, Haines Bluff, and Chattanooga. And like many other veterans when the peace finally came, he headed as far away from the crowded East as he could get. He became a mail contractor.

Running a mail route between California and "civilization" wasn't easy. There weren't many roads, Natives fought the intrusion of whites into their territories with ferocious intensity, and one could never be sure of a reliable water source. But William embodied the determination of the Western pioneer. He helped establish, managed, and later owned what became known as the Texas and California Stage Company, running passengers and the U.S. Mail between Fort Worth and San Diego. Their main stage line ran 1,700 miles in each direction and required 1,200 horses to operate. William administered the company for eight years, which was initially headquartered in San Diego, then Yuma, and finally Tucson.

He married a Southern belle named Miss Dora Fleming of Macon, Georgia in 1870 and established a home in Fort Smith, Arkansas, traveling to Fort Worth as needed. They had one son, E.E. Griffith. Dora died in 1874. In 1878, William moved with his son to the stage line's headquarters in Tucson.

There were strongly enforced rules to riding the stage:

* Abstinence from liquor is requested, but if you must drink share the bottle. To do otherwise makes you appear selfish and unneighborly.
* If ladies are present, gentlemen are urged to forego smoking cigars and pipes as the odor of same is repugnant to the gentler sex. Chewing tobacco is permitted, but spit with the wind, not against it.
* Gentlemen must refrain from the use of rough language in the presence of ladies and children.
* Buffalo robes are provided for your comfort in cold weather. Hogging robes will not be tolerated and the offender will be made to ride with the driver.
* Don't snore loudly while sleeping or use your fellow passenger's shoulder for a pillow, he or she may not understand and friction may result.
* Firearms may be kept on your person for use in emergencies. Do not fire them for pleasure or shoot at wild animals as the sound riles the horses.
* In the event of runaway horses remain calm. Leaping from the coach in panic will leave you injured, at the mercy of the elements, hostile Indians and hungry coyotes.
* Forbidden stagecoach topics of conversation are: stagecoach robberies and Indian uprisings.
* Gents guilty of unchivalrous behavior toward lady passengers will be put off the stage. It's a long walk back. A word to the wise is sufficient.

The arrival of the railroad in Tucson in 1880 rang the death knell for stagecoach passenger revenue. William wisely sold the company in 1881 and began life anew as a cattle rancher at Dripping Spring, one hundred miles north of Tucson in Gila County, Arizona Territory. He raised Shorthorn and Hereford cattle, dabbled in mining, and ran short local stage lines. William sent E.E. to Christian Brothers College in St. Louis, Missouri. E.E. also later attended the agricultural college in Fort Collins, Colorado, and became a copper miner in Morenci.

Always a Republican, William became a delegate to the party's national convention at Minneapolis in 1892 and thereafter served as a member of the National Republican Committee for nearly thirty years. A Mason and Elk, he remained involved and prominent in the Tucson community. He was appointed United States Marshal of Arizona by President William McKinley in July 1897 and served in that capacity until 1901. One of his first assignments as U.S. Marshal of Arizona dealt with what became known as The Great Grants Caper, a spectacular train robbery at Grants Station, near the Arizona-New Mexico border. Marshal Griffith was told to not to involve the U.S. Marshals because train robbery was not a federal offense—unless there was theft or destruction of the United States Mail. Pursuit of the criminals was also hindered by lack of cooperation from the Mexican authorities when gangs escaped across the border. Despite such limitations, Griffith's reputation reflected how he "discharged the duties of that office in a most commendable and satisfactory manner."

William M. Griffith left the Territory after his term expired and died in Los Angeles, California on September 2, 1922.

Ben and Lewis Williams

"Money Making Mine Management"

Cactus Cymry

Lewis Williams (standing, far left) and Ben Williams (seated, fourth from left, black bow tie), Managers of the Copper Queen Mine, Bisbee
Courtesy of the Arizona Historical Society, Tucson
#PC74_48296

Ben and Lewis Williams

Arizona's assets have long been described as "The Three C's: Cotton, Copper, and Cattle." The richest C—Copper—might not have been as prominent or as profitable to the Territory without three special Ws: John, Ben, and Lewis Williams.

John Williams (no relation to our previously identified stone mason, John S. Williams) was born approximately 1820 in Swansea, Wales, and is credited in some reference sources with developing the water-jacket blast furnace in Norway in 1852. Circulating water between the furnace wall and the well containing the ore reduced the risk of explosion and eliminated the use of firebrick. Such brick was expensive and difficult to transport in the American West and Southwest before the completion of the railroad networks. Therefore, not only did this innovative smelter work more efficiently at reaching higher temperatures without blowing up, it was far easier to construct in remote locations.

Eldest son Lewis was born in 1835 and is listed in the 1851 Census of Wales in St. Mary, Swansea, Glamorganshire in the household of John Williams. Ben was born February 27, 1852 in London, England; later that same year his father was in Norway working on the water jacket furnace. John Williams brought his family to America in 1858 and settled in Michigan for a time, moving westward to Utah after the Civil War when the transcontinental railroad was completed.

There is some confusion about whether John Williams had a son also named John. *Cochise County Stalwarts* states in one paragraph that Lewis was the eldest child born in 1835 in Swansea, and that John Jr. was born in 1845 in Swansea, but this author could not find a child named John listed in the 1851 Census in the same household as Lewis, who would have been sixteen. *A History of American Mining* states that John Williams, instrumental in making the copper mines in Globe organized and profitable, was the father of Ben and Lewis, not their brother.

"John Williams" is not exactly a rare name in Wales. But in that country at that time it was not the usual custom to use "Junior" for a son named for his father. The old Welsh custom of naming a son through several generations was cut short by the English: Thomas ap Thomas ap Robert—Thomas, a son of Thomas who was the son of Robert—became Thomas Thomas. Therefore the majority of Welsh family surnames are generally first names such as Roberts, Thomas, Edwards, Davies, Llewelyn, Hughes, Evans, and of course, Williams. Once in America though, second-generation *Cymry* easily adopted the use of "Junior" for their offspring.

Whether father or brother, John Williams evidently loved to travel. From Michigan he went to San Francisco in the early 1870s where he started a mining consulting business with DeWitt S. Bisbee, a railroad contractor and builder who had made a fortune filling in the marshlands around that city as its population boomed after the Gold Rush.

Lewis Williams built a water-jacket smelter in Utah in 1873; by 1879, his younger brother Ben had supervised the San Xavier mine near Tucson and was "looking after development work" in the Huachuca Mountains approximately eighty-five miles to the southeast.

It was Lewis who informed Ben of exciting malachite ore specimens from the Mule Mountains that had arrived at the offices of Bisbee, Williams & Company in San Francisco. Since he was already in the area, within a few days Ben rode up to the claim of George Warren and took samples. He sent those via Wells Fargo express stagecoach to San Francisco. When DeWitt Bisbee received the assay reports, he secured additional financial backing from Southern Pacific grading contractors Ballard and Martin and proceeded to negotiate options on Warren's claim, the Copper Queen.

In August of 1880, Lewis Williams arrived at the site and named the community "Bisbee" for his brother-in-law back at the firm in San Francisco. He freighted in "a thirty-six inch water jacket furnace, a Baker blower, two small engines, a forty h.p. boiler and a small rock crusher." The Southern Pacific had not yet built anything remotely close to the area, so everything had to be freighted by oxen from the depot at Pantano. Ben, now finished with his work in the Huachuca Mountains, soon joined him.

The ore coming out of the Copper Queen yielded a high concentration of approximately twenty-four-and-a-half percent fine copper. Things went well until the following year when James Douglas arrived as an agent for Phelps-Dodge and took over the Atlanta claim next door. For three years Douglas kept digging and losing money, but then hit into a lode that transected the Copper Queen's claim.

Litigation threatened to ensue and stop everyone from making any money. Ballard and Martin, only financially involved and never fully cognizant of the actual operations of mining, bailed when they assumed the Queen had played out. Bisbee, Williams and Company negotiated to keep their shares and the continuation of Lewis and Ben's management of the Copper Queen Consolidated Mining Company. While Douglas' aggressive acquisitions and determination to "obliterate the law of the apex" that allowed the Queen to expand into a massive mining complex, it was the Williams brothers' considerable knowledge of smelting problems and techniques that propelled the Queen into national prominence.

What happened then is incredible: From 1885 to 1930, inclusive, the Copper Queen mine yielded 29,166,780 tons of ore, from which there were extracted 2,740,752,125 pounds of copper, 99,158,282 pounds of lead, together with 20,451,071 ounces of silver and 486,690 ounces of gold. And production did not stop until the mid-1970s.

John Williams arrived in Globe in 1881 and began building smelters:

> The smelter was called the Carrie plant, because it treated siliceous ore from the Carrie claim. In order to obtain the necessary flux, Williams arranged to pay a dollar per ton for ironstone from the Old Globe outcrop, which happened to contain more copper than the Carrie ore; thus the value of the Old Globe was discovered... Then the Old Dominion smelter was built at Globe, this event marking the beginning of important copper mining operations in the district. By 1886 there were six furnaces at work in the Globe district, but they were forced into idleness at the end of that year on account of the low price of copper, which was then quoted at 11 cents per pound. In 1888 the Old Dominion company was reorganized, starting forthwith on a long and successful career. In 1892 Phelps, Dodge & Company purchased the United Globe mines, and...In 1903 the same firm obtained control of the Old Dominion.

It seems logical to conclude that the Williams' connections with James Douglas and Phelps-Dodge facilitated the company's expansion into Globe, Prescott, and other areas of the Territory. Sham claims and con schemes abounded in prospecting; the trust that developed between the Welsh mine managers and the Scot metallurgist truly laid the foundation for the Phelps-Dodge Corporation to expand into a powerhouse employer in Arizona for generations.

But the successes of the Williams family involved more than mining and money. They were respected, well-regarded, even revered. Lewis Williams received the honorary title of *Don Luis*, bestowed by the Mexican miners who considered him a benevolent *patron*, or boss. He and his beloved wife Harriet were active in the Bisbee community and raised three children: son Ben, daughter Josephine or "Josalee", and another daughter, Elizabeth.

Ben Williams developed the towns of Bisbee and Douglas, building both the Bank of Bisbee and the Bank of Douglas, then served as a director on their boards, as did Lewis.

John Williams died in January 1892, his body taken back to San Francisco by a special railroad car for burial. If he was indeed born in 1845, he would have been forty-seven years old. Considering all the knowledge and business acumen attributed to him in his dealings in San Francisco, Globe, and Prescott, it seems logical that this John Williams was, indeed, the father of Ben and Lewis. In 1892, he would have been in his seventies and far more likely to have been accorded the honor of a special rail car.

Lewis and Ben left Bisbee in 1899 and returned to the San Francisco area for a time, then both retired to Los Angeles. Lewis died at his son's home in 1907, a mere four months after the death of his Harriet. He was seventy-two.

After suffering a heart attack, Ben Williams was moved from his family home into an apartment on Wilshire Boulevard where he suffered a fatal hemorrhage on September 1, 1925. He was seventy-three. He was survived by his wife and thirteen year old son, Ben Jr. (a la the American manner.) His niece, Josalee and great nephew Lewis were also at his bedside. An anecdote of how esteemed Ben Williams had been was printed in his obituary in the *Los Angeles Times*:

> Friends who mourned his passing yesterday recalled a stirring tribute paid Mr. Williams upon his retirement from the management of the Copper Queen. His numerous associates wanted to give him some token of

their respect. They wrote to a great New York jewelry firm, describing Mr. Williams' character and asking that something suitable be designed. When the gift returned, it was a loving cup cast in pure gold. All agreed the choice was a happy one. If any one was "pure gold," it was Ben Williams, the mining men said in making the presentation.

As a historical note, Lewis' daughter Josalee married James Douglas, Jr., son of the Phelps-Dodge metallurgist. They had a son in 1894 they named Lewis Williams Douglas, who went on to attend Amherst College and Massachusetts Institute of Technology, became a war hero in World War I, a state senator, deputy administrator of the War Shipping Administration during World War II, and Ambassador to the Court of St. James (aka the U.S. Ambassador to Great Britain) in 1947.

Influential *Cymry*, indeed.

Other Characters of Note

Other Characters of Note

WILLIAM MORGAN

This hapless fellow was captured robbing the Wells Fargo Express stage between Prescott and Maricopa in 1879. He wasn't too imaginative when it came to aliases: "Dave Jenkins," "Dave Williams," or "Dave Jones" certainly didn't deflect anyone from looking for a Welshman. What is described about him is that his "nativity" was Wales (no town or shire specified) and he was a brick maker by supposed trade. He was forty-seven years old at the time of his apprehension, so he had been born in 1832. Morgan was light-complexioned, had blue eyes, sandy gray hair, and he stood five foot, eleven inches tall. He must have had some prior dishonest activity for all the aliases he used because this arrest was definitely his last. His partner, Thomas Francis (no description available about him at all), was shot "while resisting arrest" by the Wells Fargo armed messenger. William—or "Dave" as he seemed to prefer—was sentenced to spend the rest of his life in Yuma Territorial Prison. The take from the stage robbery? Less than $300.

JUDGE EBENEZER WILLIAMS

Judge Ebenezer Williams, a member of the bench and bar of Nogales, was a criminal attorney of highly probable Welsh descent. A native of Pittsburgh Pa., Judge Williams was born October 3, 1830, and was a son of Ebenezer and Margaret (Jones) Williams (which is about as Welsh-sounding as it gets). He attended Allegheny College in Meadville, Pennsylvania (hometown of Josephine Brawley Hughes).

When the Civil War began, he enlisted in the 101st Regiment of the Pennsylvania Volunteers (the same regiment as L.C. Hughes) as a first lieutenant, serving in the Army of the Potomac. After the war he returned to Pittsburgh until 1880 when he moved to San Diego, California. In 1884 he came to the Arizona Territory and practiced law in Mohave County where he was elected District Attorney, serving for two years. He moved his law practice to Nogales in 1891 and was appointed probate judge and superintendent of schools when Santa Cruz County was created out of the vast expanse of Pima Country in 1898. He spoke fluent Spanish and was renowned as "one of the most delightful as well as forceful extemporaneous speakers in the Territory. Judge Williams has at his command an extensive vocabulary, a ready and fine wit, and an elegance of expression, which is convincing, pleasing, and altogether acceptable." Judge Williams was a stanch Republican and a member of the Methodist Episcopal Church.

ALFRED B. WILLIAMS

Alfred Williams owned the largest catering establishment in the territory in 1901. On West Washington Street in Phoenix, his building was one of the few with a "cold storage plant, wherein is manufactured the ice necessary for the carrying on of the business." Though Alfred was born in Ipswich, Suffolk, England, on August 21, 1862, his paternal grandfather came from Wales, settled in Worcestershire, was educated as a clergyman in the Church of England, graduated in *belles letters,* and was elected to the chair of classics at Cambridge University. Alfred's father, Thomas, was born in Worcestershire and died young.

Mr. Williams relocated to Phoenix in 1891, started a small restaurant, and was so successful he expanded into the large catering business mentioned above. He was a Republican and attended the Episcopal Church.

Other Characters of Note

WILLIAM G. DAVIS

Born in Wales, November 24, 1841, William G. Davis immigrated to America when he was thirteen years old, and fended for himself from then on. For some time he lived in Iowa, subsequently going to Utah, where he dwelt chiefly in Salt Lake County. As soon as he had sufficient money to provide for his parents, John and Elizabeth (Cadwallader) Davis, he sent for them, "and continued to minister to their needs until they were called to the silent land."

In 1892 William came to Lehi (present day Mesa, southeast Phoenix) to homestead and created once of the most profitable farms in the valley. In political matters he was a Democrat and a member of the Church of Jesus Christ of the Latter-day Saints, and besides serving as a superintendent of the Sunday-school and in other official positions, he went to England on a two-year ecclesiastical mission in 1880.

The first marriage of Mr. Davis occurred in Utah to Esther Harrison, a native of England. "For a second wife Mr. Davis chose Miss Emily Nix, likewise of England." He fathered a total of fourteen children and died in 1900 at the age of fifty-nine.

HON. JOHN S. JONES

Mr. Jones was born in Wales (there is no specification of where) and immigrated with his parents in 1861 to Columbus, Ohio. He was apprenticed as a machinist, serving four years, then was assistant engineer at the Deaf and Dumb Institute of Columbus. In 1870 he moved to St. Louis, Missouri, manufacturing mining machinery with the firm Ferguson & Jones. He started in mining operations in the Black Hills of Dakota in 1879, continued in Central America and Colorado before arriving in Arizona's Yavapai County in 1888.

Devoting his time to prospecting for himself, he located the Little Jessie mine in 1889, and continued to make claims at points which he deemed worthy of being developed. The Little Jessie group ultimately comprised eighteen claims mainly mining gold and silver, allowing Mr. Jones to rapidly amass a fortune.

John S. Jones was elected to the territorial legislature in the eighteenth general assembly (hence the honorific title) as a stalwart Republican.

WILLIAM THOMAS

"When a babe in arms Mr. Thomas was brought by his parents from the little country of Wales" (no town or shire specified) to near Canton, Ohio. Mr. Thomas was superintendent of the Yavapai County Hospital in Prescott from 1895 through 1898, then again from 1900 through 1901. As a young man he came to Arizona and engaged in mining in 1889, raising cattle and hogs as well, and invested in property all around the Prescott area. Mr. Thomas was a Republican, and "a great admirer of President McKinley, whom he has the honor to personally know. A large share of his success is generously and fairly attributed to the earnest efforts of his wife, whom he married in July, 1885, and who was formerly Anna Brown, of North Lawrence, Ohio." They had four children, three of whom had died by 1901.

MARSHALL WILLIAMS

The name is often associated with Tombstone legend, but Marshall Williams has been a slippery eel to research. There is no readily found information on his background other than he was born in New York about 1852. So this author has no

Other Characters of Note

definitive evidence to verify that he was of Welsh descent, other than his name. But he's an interesting character, as many *Cymry* in the Old West were, so here's a bit of the story:

In 1880 Marshall Williams was the Well Fargo Express Agent/ Station Manager for Tombstone. He received ten percent of the tariffs on stagecoach tickets out of Tombstone, predominantly to towns such as Tucson, Benson, and Bisbee. Like most agents of the day, he supplemented his income selling cigars, tobacco, newspapers, and candy. He was a friend of the Earp faction and the "resident correspondent" for the *Boston Economist*.

He was also a con man, gambler, and embezzler. Marshall Williams cooked the books of the Wells Fargo Station, and allegedly often gave stagecoach cargo information to a group of outlaws for a cut of the haul, the most famous of which resulted in the death of stage driver Bud Philpot in March of 1881. Wild rumor mongers on the streets of Tombstone intimated Doc Holliday had possibly set up the robbery to have the armed messenger Bob Paul killed so Morgan Earp could then take over his position.

This rumor is pretty much another fabrication that merely adds to the overabundance of fertilizer that fuels many Old West myths and legends in Tombstone. Morgan Earp had already served Wells Fargo as a shotgun messenger, as their cash books attest. Bob Paul was riding the coach as a messenger only until he could be seated as Sheriff of Pima County; he'd been elected to that office in November 1880. This was the famous election in which the Clantons and their buddies stuffed the San Simon ballot box to elect Paul's opponent, Charles Shibell. Paul had exposed the fraud and Shibell's election was overturned in court in January of 1881. Paul was awaiting the conclusion of Shibell's appeal when he rode that Benson stage. It was his last run as a Wells Fargo Armed Messenger. He pinned on the Sheriff's badge in April 1881, after Shibell's appeal was denied, and went on to serve seven consecutive terms.

In any case, shots in the dark as the stage robbery ensued took Philpot's life and started dominoes falling that ultimately culminated in the legendary Gunfight at the OK Corral in October of 1881—or so the story goes.

Fred Dodge, in the guise of a gambler, had been hired by Wells Fargo's General Superintendent John J. Valentine to go to Tombstone in 1880 in an undercover operation independent of the regular detective department run by James B. Hume and John Thacker.

Dodge watched the popular Williams operate in Tombstone and sent word to Valentine in San Francisco that something wasn't quite right about the frequency of stage robberies and Williams' high rolling sprees at the faro tables. Seems he threw around more money than even an extremely industrious Wells Fargo Agent could make.

But in February of 1882, as Wells Fargo detectives were closing in, Marshall Williams slipped away with "a sport of questionable character" (another of those wonderful nineteenth century euphemisms for prostitute) and headed for parts unknown. He left "a multitude of five-cent cigars and toys," as well as "about $8,000 of unpaid debts behind him as a kind of remembrance." His whereabouts for remainder of his life remain unknown. He was never seen in Tombstone again.

An ironic side note: In January 1882, head of the Wells Fargo Detectives James B. Hume was on a stagecoach just outside of Tombstone when he was "relieved of a fine set of pistols, a watch, and his money" as the stage was robbed. There's no evidence to indicate Marshall Williams had set that one up, but Hume stayed on in Tombstone to hunt for the robbers. Purely coincidental that Williams skipped town only a few weeks later.

Epilogue

The Flag of Wales: Y Ddraig Goch (Photo by J. Johnson)

Epilogue

Quite possibly, there have been many more Welsh immigrants to the wild Arizona Territory who lived quiet lives, going about the business of survival in a hostile desert environment. Many disappeared into the woodwork, never mentioning their origins. Illegal immigration was less of a concern then as the powers that ran the Territory were happy to get every white person they could as residents.

As stated before, there were no concentrated Welsh communities in Arizona such as those near the coal mines of Pennsylvania, West Virginia, and other Eastern states. But in Bisbee, known for being a "White Camp" where miners and their families were strictly segregated by race and nationality, the Welsh tended to live on the south side of the town, near the Italians and Irish. The English, Scots, and Swedes commanded the hilltops, and the Mexicans and swarthy Eastern Europeans were kept to the bottom of Brewery Gulch—where all the sewage ran. No African-Americans were permitted within the town limits of Bisbee after sunset, even the famed Buffalo Soldiers Cavalry stationed at nearby Fort Huachuca to defend the town from Geronimo and his warriors. In fact, one soldier who had spent the day chasing Apaches away from Bisbee was nearly beaten to death when he didn't get out of town fast enough. One would hope things have changed by now.

Con men, stage robbers, shrewd businessmen, and of course, mining experts—the immigrants from The Land of Song left their mark on the history of the Grand Canyon State. One just has to look closely to recognize the footprints of *Y Ddraig Goch*—the Red Dragon—the national symbol of Wales.

Reference Notes

What Brought Them Here

1. "A country fit only for Apaches, snakes, and other Queer Reptiles": Mrs. Opie Rundle Brugess Lea, personal records, Arizona Historical Society.

2. The industrialization of the South Wales Valleys; http://www.data-wales.co.uk /valley1.htm

3. Each landowner could add tollgates wherever a road crossed or abutted his property to cover the costs for maintenance and repair. Collectors —"Toll farmers"—bid for the privilege to take delivery of these fees. The Rebecca Riots; http://www.nationalarchives.gov.uk/education/lesson48.htm

4. From 1839 till 1845, the *Merched Beca*—Daughters of Rebecca—took inspiration from the Boston Tea Party and organized to destroy toll gates during ever more aggressive acts of civil disobedience that ultimately necessitated the creation of a police force for southern Wales. *The Rebecca Riots* by David Williams, University of Wales Press, 1986. http://www.data-wales.co.uk/emig1.htm

5. "In America, radicals freed from inhibition could voice opinions only hinted at in Wales." *Beginnings of Radicalism P.2; The Remaking of Wales in the Eighteenth Century*, Professor Gwyn Alf Williams of Cardiff University. http://openlearn.open.ac.uk/mod/oucontent/view.php?id=397309&section=2.1.6

Samuel Hughes

1. Clifford J. Stratton...admits "may be a little slanted toward our family's point of view." Hughes Family History by Clifford J. Stratton; Samuel Hughes Papers; Arizona Historical Society.

2. "Sam Hughes, First Booster;" *Tucson Citizen*; April 15, 1915.

3. "after having been fascinated by the corn sailors brought back from this area. He had a large family and decided the new country seemed like a land of opportunity." Plaza of the Pioneers booklet P.15.

4. The estate in Wales: *Portrait and Biographical Record of Arizona;* Chapman Publishing Co., Chicago, 1901, P.67. http://www.archive.org/stream/portraitbioarizo00chaprich/ portraitbioarizo00chaprich_djvu.txt.

5. "But we were all the same blood and I could get along without it." "Sam Hughes, Dean of Tucson Pioneers, Dies"; *Tucson Citizen*, June 20 1917.

6. The family immigrated on the "North Star," a sailing vessel whose voyage lasted sixty days. "Sam Hughes, Dean of Tucson Pioneers, Dies"; *Tucson Citizen*, June 20, 1917.

7. Sallie Hughes might have been born aboard the "North Star" on the voyage to America, but her headstone indicates she was born in 1838: http://genealogy.drnewcomb.ftml.net/b149.htm

8. "*David*, a prominent man of New Orleans, La., where his death occurred; Mrs. *Sally (or Sallie)* Taylor and [older sister Lizzie], both residents of DeSoto, Kans.; *William*, who was a member of a Kansas regiment in the Civil war and is now a resident of Lawrence, that state; [Thomas]; and *Annie*, who makes her home in Tucson." *Portrait and Biographical Record of Arizona;* Chapman Publishing Co., Chicago, 1901; P.67. http://www.archive.org/stream/portraitbioarizo00chaprich/ portraitbioarizo00chaprich_djvu.txt

9. 1860 Census: http://genealogy.drnewcomb.ftml.net/b149.htm: 1860 Census, Penn., Allegheny, population, South Fayette, Mt. Lebanon, p. 73, Samuel Hughes, line 25.

Reference Notes

10. Sam mentions him only in passing, to note that man died at the age of seventy. "Sam Hughes, First Booster;" *Tucson Citizen*; April 15, 1915.

11. Sam stated in numerous interviews that he "strained his chest lifting the carcass of a deer onto his horse. Something slipped and he was badly hurt" in 1857 and the doctors told him to seek a warmer climate or he would die. "Sam Hughes, Dean of Tucson Pioneers, Dies"; *Tucson Citizen*, June 20 1917.

12. Sam "compelled to leave California for the milder climate of Arizona, being, at that time, in the last stages of tuberculosis." *History of Arizona, Volume II;* Thomas Edwin Farish; The Filmer Brothers Electrotype Company, San Francisco, 1915; P. 210. http://southwest.library.arizona.edu/hav2/body.1_div.10.html

13. "The lungers will never get well by lying around doing nothing. They want to get interested in something like I did." "Sam Hughes, First Booster;" *Tucson Citizen*; April 15, 1915.

14. In fact, "Secesh" delegates met in Tucson in 1860: *The Civil War in Arizona / New Mexico Territory;* http://www.discoverseaz.com/History/Civil_War.html

15. Definition of Accessory: http://dictionary.law.com/Default.aspx?selected=2300

16. Quote by historian Howard Sheldon: http://www.desertusa.com/mag98/april/stories/campgrant1.html

17. Camp Grant's surgeon documented the "grisly sight of corpses left to rot in the sun." http://www.desertusa.com/mag98/april/stories/campgrant1.html

18. "swift punishment was dealt out to those red-handed butchers, and they were wiped from the face of the earth." "The Pioneers; The Story of the Camp Grant Massacre of 1871, Retold by the Captain of the Expedition to His Old Comrades--Interesting Historical Data Worth Preserving." http://dl.lib.brown.edu/repository2/repoman.php?verb=render_xslt&id=1227191036875000.xml&view=1226416901875000.xsl&colid=55

18. Historian C.L. Sonnichsen writes, "The pioneers deserve to be judged by their own standards and beliefs, not by ours, and in their view…they *had* brought civilization of a sort to the new country and had risked their lives to do it." *Pioneer Heritage*, C.L. Sonnichsen; Arizona Historical Society, 1984; p.5.

19. Carrillo and Hughes had already achieved what they wanted: the small farms had failed and Hughes had bought their properties for pennies on the dollar, then turned around and leased them to Chinese farmers. Hadley, D. & Speelman, M, "Don Leopoldo Carrillo: Sonoran Merchant and Developer in Territorial Tucson"; Arizona History Convention, 2006.

20. Sam Hughes…was later praised for "providing excellent soil for skilled Chinese farmers." *Tucson Was a Railroad Town*; .P. 266; Kalt, William D III; VTD Rail Publishing, Mountlake Terrace, WA; 2007.

21. On May 1, 1872, Sam Hughes created a mortgage for them for the amount of $330.00 that was discharged by July 1873. Pima Country Recorder, Book 1: p. 245-7. Tucson, Arizona.

22. 1901 glowing summary: *Portrait and Biographical Record of Arizona;* Chapman Publishing Co., Chicago, 1901; P. 67-70. http://www.archive.org/stream/portraitbioarizo00chaprich / portraitbioarizo00chaprich _djvu.txt

Reference Notes

23. He cautioned Editor John Wasson to never mention his involvement by name. Interview in the *Tucson Citizen*, April 1915.

24. All quotes by Sam in this section: Interview in the *Tucson Citizen*, April 1915; Chapter IV, p. 17.

James Daly

1. "One of the most celebrated crimes in the annals of Arizona history." *Cochise County Stalwarts*, Lynn R. Bailey & Don Chaput ; Westernlore Pr; January 2000; P. 82.

2. Jones saw nothing more than "copper-stained rock". *A History of American Mining*; Thomas Arthur Rickard, author; McGraw-Hill, 1932; P. 283; www.archive.org/details/AHistoryOfAmericanMining

3. Mining information regarding the Copper Queen in this section: "History of the Phelps-Dodge Corporation"; http://www.phelpsdodge.com

4. The "rule of the apex," according to which a claim owner could follow a vein of ore onto another claim, if the deposit had come closest to the surface on his land. "History of the Phelps-Dodge Corporation"; http://www.phelpsdodge.com

5. Apex or extralateral rights and the Copper Queen: "The Law in Tombstone: Mining Camp Jurisprudence, 1879- 1886"; Robert F. Palmquist, Arizona Historical Society, 2004.

5. Physical description of James Daly and incident with Deputies Simmons and Lowther: *Cochise County Stalwarts*, Lynn R. Bailey & Don Chaput ; Westernlore Pr; January 2000; P. 82.

6. "Suddenly, through a window came a flash and a report and Lowther fell, shot through the heart by an unseen assassin. When found, the murdered officer still had between his teeth the toothpick he had been chewing when so suddenly stricken." *The Arizona Daily Gazette*, January 24, 1895.

7. W.W. Lowther Obituary: http://files.usgwarchives.net/az/cochise/obits/lowther.txt

8. Complications arose when a German woman ...to come to Bisbee. *Cochise County Stalwarts*, Lynn R. Bailey & Don Chaput ; Westernlore Pr; January 2000; P. 82.

9. Description of legal situation with Costello and Phelp-Dodge: *A History of American Mining*, Thomas Rickard, copyright 1932; P. 284; www.archive.org/details/AHistoryOfAmericanMining

10. Description of Daly's demise: *Cochise County Stalwarts*, Lynn R. Bailey & Don Chaput, authors; Westernlore Pr; copyright January 2000; P. 83.

John S. Williams

1. 1871 Census of Wales; http://ancestry.com

2. Great Registry of Cochise County, 1884.

3. Bisbee Mining Museum Archives; Cemetery Records/Map, P.3, section 12.

Louis Cameron Hughes

1. Louis became an indentured servant at age ten to devout Calvinist farmer Samuel Alter: http://genealogy.drnewcomb.

Reference Notes

ftml.net/b149.htm; 1860 Census, Penn., Allegheny, population, South Fayette, Mt. Lebanon; P. 73.

2. John Calvin (1509-1564) theology: *Calvinism in a Nutshell*; http://www.insearchoftruth.org/articles/calvinism.html

3. "given $15 and sent out into the world." http://jeff.scott.tripod.com/Hughes.html

4. "the orphan boy had read Uncle Tom's Cabin, and taking part in the school debates, was ardent for the freedom of black boys and girls." *Arizona The Youngest State*; James H. McClintock, 1916; Vol III, Page 6 – 12.

5. Louis was discharged in North Carolina after eighteen months due to a life-threatening case of dysentery. Louis C. Hughes Certificate of Disability Discharge, Army of the United States; AZ Historical Society file WC816617.

6. L. C. Hughes' life prior to arriving in Arizona: *Arizona The Youngest State*; James H. McClintock, 1916; Vol III; pp 6-12.

7. The effect the arrival of white "American" women had in the West: *Western Women: Their Land, Their Lives*; Lillian Schlissel, Vicki L. Ruiz, Janice Monk (Editors); University of New Mexico Press, October 1988.

8. Inset quote: *Portrait and Biographical Record of Arizona;* Chapman Publishing Co., Chicago; 1901; P.22. http://www.archive.org/stream/portraitbioarizo00chaprich/portraitbioarizo00chaprich_djvu.txt

9. Crook and Miles reactions to Apache relocations: Robert Wooster, *Nelson Miles & The Twilight of the Frontier Army*; University of Nebraska Press,1993; pp. 148-156. [Thank you, Robert F. Palmquist.]

10. Geronimo; "1918 Letter Claims Geronimo's Bones Found"; Stephen Singer, (The Associated Press, May 8, 2006); http://www.washingtonpost.com/wp-dyn/content/article/2006/05/08/AR2006050801301.html

11. L.C.'s legal accomplishments and legislative work, including Indian water rights recommendations: *Arizona The Youngest State*; James H. McClintock, 1916; Vol III, pp 6–12.

12. Stint and resignation as Attorney General: "Disgracing An Official," The *Tucson Citizen* May 22, 1905.

13. Appointment to Territorial Governor by President Grover Cleveland: "He Has Got It"; *Tucson Citizen*, April 6, 1893.

14. "Skinning a Skunk", *Tucson Citizen* May 22, 1905.

15. Governor Hughes' fiscal accomplishments: *Arizona The Youngest State*; James H. McClintock, 1916; Vol III; pp 6–12.

William M. Griffith

1. Information about William Griffith from *Portrait and Biographical Record of Arizona;* Chapman Publishing Co., Chicago; 1901; pp. 57-58. http://www.archive.org/stream/portraitbioarizo00chaprich/portraitbioarizo00chaprich_djvu.txt

2. Stagecoach Rules quoted from Elizabeth C. MacPhail, "Wells Fargo in San Diego," *The Journal of San Diego History*, Fall 1980, Volume 28, Number 4.

3. *Last of the Old-Time Outlaws: The George West Musgrave Story,* Karen H. Tanner and John D. Tanner Jr., Authors; University of Oklahoma Press, 2002; p. 144.

Reference Notes

4. Quote from *Portrait and Biographical Record of Arizona;* 1901; P.58.
http://www.archive.org/stream/portraitbioarizo00chaprich/portraitbioarizo00chaprich_djvu.txt

5. Griffith, William M.: Obituary, *The Arizona Daily Star*, September 5, 1922.

Ben and Lewis Williams

1. *The Metallurgy of Lead and the Desilverization of Base Bullion*; Heinrich Oscar Hofman, Author; Hill Publishing Co., 1904, Edition 7; p. 243.

2. Ancestry.co.uk: 1851 Census of Wales; Baptismal record of Ben Williams, 1852.

3. *Cochise County Stalwarts*, Lynn R. Bailey & Don Chaput ; Westernlore Pr., 2000; pp.188-189.

4. *A History of American Mining*; Thomas Arthur Rickard, author; McGraw-Hill, 1932; P.283.

5. Williams, Ben: Tribute; *Bisbee Daily Review*, September 10, 1925

6. Statistics of the yield of the Copper Queen Mine: *A History of American Mining*; Thomas Arthur Rickard, author; McGraw-Hill, 1932; P.285.

7. Inset quote: *A History of American Mining*; Thomas Arthur Rickard, author; McGraw-Hill, 1932; P.292.

8. Lewis Williams family information: *Cochise County Stalwarts*, Lynn R. Bailey & Don Chaput; Westernlore Pr., 2000; P. 190.

9. Information regarding Lewis Williams Douglas: *Independent: A Biography of Lewis W. Douglas;* Robert Paul Browder and Thomas G. Smith, authors; Alfred A. Knopf, 1986; pps. 241-328.

10. "Pioneer Mine Head Dies: Ben Williams, Prominent in Western Development and Banking Affairs, Passes Here;" *Los Angeles Times,* September 3, 1925.

Other Characters of Note

William Morgan:
Report of Jas. B. Hume and Jno. N. Thacker, special officers, Wells, Fargo & Co's Express: covering a period of fourteen years : giving losses by train robbers, stage robbers and burglaries: and a full description and record of all noted criminals convicted of offenses against Wells, Fargo & Company since November 5th, 1870; Hume, James B. and Thacker, John N..; Wells, Fargo & Co., San Francisco CA, 1885.

For these *Cymry,* little else is written but for an overly gushing blurb in the 1,044 page tome published in 1901, *Portrait and Biographical Record of Arizona*: "Commemorating the achievements of citizens who have contributed to the progress of Arizona and the development of its resources." Additional research to confirm or disprove information presented here is needed; they have been included only in passing as Welsh immigrants or of probable Welsh descent whose accomplishments in Arizona have faded from public knowledge over the past 100 years. They should be remembered.

Portrait and Biographical Record of Arizona; Chapman Publishing Co., Chicago; 1901; http://www.archive.org/stream/portraitbioarizo00chaprich/portraitbioarizo00chaprich_djvu.txt

Reference Notes

Judge Ebenezer Williams: pp.161-162.

Hon. William Morgan: p. 207.

Alfred B. Williams: pp. 508-511.

William G. Davis: p. 533.

Hon John S. Jones: p. 559

William Thomas: p. 681

Marshall Williams:
1. *Cochise County Stalwarts*, Lynn R. Bailey & Don Chaput; Westernlore Pr., 2000; P. 190.

2. *Report of Jas. B. Hume and Jno. N. Thacker, special officers, Wells, Fargo & Co's Express: covering a period of fourteen years : giving losses by train robbers, stage robbers and burglaries: and a full description and record of all noted criminals convicted of offenses against Wells, Fargo & Company since November 5th, 1870;* Hume, James B. and Thacker, John N..; Wells, Fargo & Co., San Francisco CA, 1885.

About the Author

About the Author

Jude Johnson has been a history enthusiast since childhood and has lectured about her historical research at the Sierra Vista Historical Society, the Welsh League of Arizona, and the West Coast Eisteddfod in Los Angeles.

She is the author of the *Dragon & Hawk* series of novels set in the Arizona Territory that follow three fictional brothers from Wales from the copper mines of Bisbee to the gambling halls of Tombstone and the growing community of Tucson. Four years of historical research preceded the completion of the first novel. *Dragon & Hawk* is published by Champagne Books (http://www.champagnebooks.com) with two sequels set for publication in 2012.

She is a member of Gecko Gals Ink, LLC, a group of "sassy Tucson authors" who encourage other writers to become published by holding writing seminars and classes.

Jude grew up in Western Pennsylvania. Her father's family settled in the Meadville area prior to the Revolutionary War. Her mother's family came from Nogales, Sonora, Mexico, and immigrated to Tucson in the early twentieth century. (The condensation Josephine and L.C. Hughes showed towards their Mexican sister-in-law was all too similar to descriptions of how Jude's paternal grandmother initially treated her mother.) Allegheny College, alma mater of Judge Ebenezer Williams, was also the alma mater of Jude's father and older brother.

Jude attended Dickinson College in Carlisle, Pennsylvania and Sherman College of Chiropractic in Spartanburg, South Carolina. She moved to Tucson after completing her education as a Chiropractic Physician and has been in continual practice since 1981, and plans to keep her day job for the foreseeable future. While she has no Welsh heritage in her lineage, she has studied *Cymraeg* and learned just enough to be dangerous in Cardiff pubs. She also speaks bad border Spanish that gets better with *cerveza*.

Cactus Cymry

    She lives in the foothills of the Santa Catalina Mountains with her long-suffering husband and son, who have resigned themselves to ingesting charred food while she's in a writing frenzy.

Website:
http://jude-johnson.com
Facebook:
http://www.facebook.com/JudeJohnsonAZ
Blogs:
http://wordsthatremain.blogspot.com
http://geckogalsink.blogspot.com
http://thewritersvineyard.blogspot.com

www.ingramcontent.com/pod-product-compliance
Lightning Source LLC
Chambersburg PA
CBHW031257290426
44109CB00012B/617